The Crisis in Teacher Education:
A European Concern?

Anthony Adams
and
Witold Tulasiewicz

 The Falmer Press

(A member of the Taylor & Francis Group)
London • Washington, D.C.

UK   The Falmer Press, 4 John Street, London WC1N 2ET
USA   The Falmer Press, Taylor & Francis Inc., 1900 Frost Road, Suite 101,
      Bristol, PA 19007

First published in 1995

A catalogue record for this book is available from the British Library

Library of Congress Cataloging-in-Publication Data are available on request

ISBN 0 7507 0284 2 cased
ISBN 0 7507 0285 0 paper

Jacket design by Caroline Archer

Typeset in 10.5/12pt Bembo by
Graphicraft Typesetters Ltd., Hong Kong.

Printed in Great Britain by Burgess Science Press, Basingstoke on paper which has a specified pH value on final paper manufacture of not less than 7.5 and is therefore 'acid free'.

The Crisis in Teacher Education

This book is

Contents

Contents

Acknowledgments

In the writing of this book the authors have been greatly helped by the advice and information provided by many people. Notable amongst these, whose assistance we would especially like to mention, are:

Dan Taverner, OBE and former chief inspector of schools for the London Borough of Newham; Conor Galvin, who is conducting research in Cambridge into the articled teachers' scheme; Andrew Convey, University of Leeds; Tony Male and Bill Musk of the Central Bureau for School Visits and Exchanges: and the work of the European Regional Partnership.

In Scotland we were cordially received and illuminated by John Mitchell, OBE of the Scottish Education Department and his colleagues; Ivor Sutherland, registrar of the General Teaching Council for Scotland; the deputy director of Jordanhill College, together with Bryan Peck and his colleagues also at Jordanhill; Gordon Liddell at Moray House; and Sydney Smyth, formerly director of the Centre for Information on the Teaching of English.

For overseas advice and help we are obliged to Linda Darling-Hammond, Teachers' College, New York; Friedrich Kron, University of Mainz; Gilles Ferry, University of Nanterre; François Audigier, Institut National de Recherche Pédagogique; and Stanisław Zabielski, University of Warsaw and his colleagues in the Białystok *kuratorium*.

For bibliographical assistance our thanks are due to Sheila Hakin, librarian in the Department of Education, University of Cambridge and to the staff of the United Kingdom Centre for European Education. We are also grateful to John Cairns for compiling the Index and to Jackie Day for her support and Editorial skills.

Introduction

The book draws attention to some current problems which face the teaching profession. In England deficiencies in teachers' knowledge have been cited, in the words of a survey conducted by Her Majesty's Inspectorate (HMI, 1988), 'initial training courses are not geared to the needs of . . . schools', while in the United States Goodlad (1991) has criticized teacher training for 'incoherent programmes not tied to a mission, with no basic principles of curriculum guiding them, no organizing themes or elements'.

In the course of political debate the deficiencies seem to have attracted more public attention when linked to a supposed fall in education standards generally, rather than as a direct result of investigations of the situation in teacher-training institutions, the feedback from which has in fact not all been bad (OFSTED, 1993). Less urgently, the socio-economic challenges presented by the realities of the European union have also been responsible for calls to raise standards of educational performance and improved provision in member states. Be that as it may, in Britain, where the Conservative Government is engaged in 'revitalising its moribund education programme' the issue of radical reform in the words of *The Times* (3 May 1994) 'has been evaded for too long'.

We do, however, also cast our glances wider into mainland Europe to look at some of the reforms being implemented there, with France and Germany as especially helpful examples. Indeed many of the changes elsewhere seem to address priorities different from those reflected by the British changes, which are increasingly seen as being motivated by ideological, market considerations (Simon, 1994) and which go beyond what can be termed as *educational* improvements as such. McLean (1992) is particularly concerned when 'the European model of elaborated aims and content which teachers have been trusted to implement and assess, has been turned on its head . . .'.

After the Treaty on Union, the so-called Maastricht Treaty of 1993, with the United Kingdom having become a full member of the European union, the divergences in patterns of teacher education assume all the hallmarks of a crisis. This is because teacher preparation closely affects the education, and thus the potential European orientation, of the very generation of school pupils that will take their place as adult workers in the new Europe, where most of Britain's economic and socio-political resources are now invested. The crisis is, therefore, both a British and a European one, although, reading the British press, one could be forgiven for thinking otherwise.

Even as the 1994 Education Bill, which led to the establishment of the Teacher Training Agency (TTA), was making its way through Parliament, the perennial British cash shortage reappeared. The financial threat was added to the teacher-education reforms already questioned on grounds of professional efficiency and viability (The *Observer*, 15 May, 1994) and confirmed by the extra expense of school-centred initial teacher training over the traditional Postgraduate Certificate of Education (PGCE) model.

Warnings of slipping educational standards and of poor economic performance have come from many sides; from those affected, but only indirectly involved with education, such as parents (The National Confederation of Parent Teacher Associations), school governors (The National Association of School Governors) and business interests (The Confederation of British Industry); and from some amongst those professionally more directly involved, including teachers and inspectors, as well as government officials, with perhaps themselves to blame. Indeed, in its summary of the basis for its opposition to government proposals for the reform of teacher education, the Committee of Vice-Chancellors and Principals (CVPC) quotes the Institute for Public Policy Research as saying:

> Any idea that a satisfactory training programme could be mounted without providing the student teacher access to the resources in a conventional training department should be ruled out. 'Sitting by Nelly' has weakened British industry and would be even more out of place in professional training. (Ross and Tomlinson, 1991)

Such claims must be investigated, if the opportunities that working together efficiently throughout Europe can bring, are not to be squandered.

We write from the perspective and experience of many years of teacher education in Cambridge, having seen it go through considerable changes there alongside similar changes in the rest of the United Kingdom, with our experience widened by our involvement in continental Europe and beyond.

The book is about two things: the preparation of teachers and change. It also argues a third: that the changes in teacher preparation may result in crisis. Though it is particularly concerned with the situation in England and Wales, comments are also made with reference to other countries in membership of the European union: especially Scotland, Germany, and France.

In Poland there is currently discussion about encouraging independent teacher initiatives and curriculum reform which is to include education for Europe. In America, to be precise in the State University of Michigan, the model of the Professional Development School (PDS) has its origins, which derives directly from the Holmes proposals (Soltis, 1987). In the guise of the 'teaching hospital school' this has found much interest among educationalists in the UK, for example Mary Warnock, writing in the *Times Educational Supplement* under the title, 'Trained Relations' (21 September 1990), still echoed by David Hargreaves (1994).

Comparative study encourages reflection and may well help steer developments in teacher education in directions offering perspectives different from those currently debated.

The structure of the book is both chronological, monitoring developments up to the present, and thematic, attempting an analysis of the several components of teacher preparation. The content of teacher preparation can be divided in different ways, emphasizing subject and curriculum knowledge, or general and subject teaching pedagogy (Bennett and Carré, 1993), for example. The division made in this book distinguishes between personal and professional knowledge and skills, and deals also with the location of training and the status of personnel involved. A European component of teacher preparation is suggested. Much of the discussion is built around the structures, policies and practices of teacher preparation listed in this Introduction and put in a socio-political context in the following chapter.

Part 1 deals mainly with the situation in England and Wales, and takes a more pronounced chronological stance. This enables the current reforms, often criticized as 'bolted on additions' resulting in some instances in a 100 per cent school-based initial training, to be seen for the radical departure they are from positions achieved over the years in the development of teacher training and autonomy. They break the link between professional preparation and higher education and put unprecedented powers over teacher preparation in the hands of the Secretary of State and his nominees. In the rest of Europe change can more readily be understood as a direct response to teacher shortages and the need to provide a professional response to the challenges of the 'New Europe'.

The number of countries cited by way of comparison in Part 2 would make a chronological approach too wide for the scope of this volume. A thematic discussion of the acknowledged parts which together make up the whole of a teacher-preparation course — theory, practice and induction — is used instead.

Part 3 looks at teacher preparation in the new Europe. The component parts of a teacher-preparation course, which will be discussed in detail in the following chapters, include:

- **education**, the skills and knowledge which we call 'academic and personal education'. They can be acquired prior to entering into a teaching commitment, or concurrently with training for it;
- **transfer of academic education** to school circumstances, the

process of adapting the content of a university discipline to pupils' personal needs and school requirements, which can be acquired concurrently with the above, or be consecutive with it. This constitutes 'teaching method';

- **professional theory** which, as 'curriculum knowledge', represents much of the actual teaching matter in teacher preparation, but which, as *educational theory*, is often believed to provide little that is immediately useful for the teacher in terms of classroom skills. As an academic discipline, *educational theory* enables teachers to become aware of the general aims and practices of education. It provides the context for their future approach as teachers. As a constituent part of teachers' general socio-political and psychological education, it can help them become more aware of the opportunity to use their freedom of choice in the exercise of their profession;

- **professional preparation and practice** identifies the skills and knowledge which serve as an introduction to actual classroom teaching. During this period prospective teachers acquire and practise a full range of classroom skills, including those of classroom management.

Part 1

The Situation in Britain

Chapter 1

The General Context of Teacher Education[1]

The Content and Location of Courses

Two elements comprising teacher education: the *content*, that is the subject matter, some of which the teacher will be expected to teach, and the *method* of teaching that content can immediately be identified. The *location*, the place where content and method are taught for the specified duration of the teacher-preparation course, is the third, which is not so readily recognized. This tripartite division gives an emphasis to important aspects of teacher education not named so far.

The presence of the first element, the content of teaching, has always been explicitly acknowledged. The Roman slave who taught his young master to read had learnt the craft himself and was teaching it to his master who did not possess it. Being in possession of an identified skill and knowledge generally acknowledged to be useful, the slave was in certain respects his master's superior. Though the reading skill alone did not change the respective roles of master and slave, it is possible to think of a set of circumstances where the possession of a skill together with appropriate items of knowledge would give power to the possessor to be used to his advantage and according to his terms of interpreting this advantage.

A rabbi whose total knowledge is clearly more than a skill used in everyday, secular pursuits, can readily be perceived as a teacher whose instructions have to be obeyed, a process in which he becomes his pupil's master. This is so even though the pupil, who, as a member of his congregation, and in his religious custody, may possess an education which, in a secular context, is superior to that of the rabbi. It is important to accept this distinction in status between different kinds of knowledge when referring to the secular teacher's knowledge which only he will possess.

The second element, teaching method, has likewise always been there, although its presence has been less explicit. Teachers would use methods, crude or refined, in order efficiently, as they saw it, to teach subject matter to their pupils. In so doing, teachers would be exercising their professional skills and expertise. However, parts of this tutorial link with a pupil would often be shared with others concerned with the same 'educatee': parents, carers, nurses, priests, social workers, and officials who are also in contact

3

with the child. As a result, in the bringing up of children, the actual practices and methods of teaching have been less exclusively associated with teachers than has the school subject knowledge taught by them, enabling other interested parties, besides teachers, to lay a claim to being given a say. The somewhat blurred distinction between teaching, up-bringing and instruction, all three to be found in the context of school education, may be carried over into teacher education.

The location, where the teaching takes place, has probably been subject to at least as many changes as the knowledge and skills which make up the content and method of education. These three elements, separately and together, constitute and affect the shape of teacher preparation.

The State and Teacher Education

Since teaching is a mass activity, which affects most people at some stage for the duration of at least a fifth of their entire lives and since most of it is controlled by the nation state, there are more factors which influence teaching than is the case with the other major professions.

Even though with over 467,000 teaching staff, excluding independent schools, employed in the United Kingdom in 1989/90 (DES Statistics, 1991b), or with some 471,000 in what was West Germany in the year before reunification (Brockhaus, 1990), teachers may indeed be outnumbered by civil servants and all other bureaucrats who together have an impact on citizens' lives, given the way compulsory education is administered, it affects everyone more closely and more directly than any other public service. That is one reason why education is so often in the news.

The nation state is concerned with the education of *all* children, whether they are educated in state schools or not, to an extent that the work of other professions is not. This situation goes back many centuries, illustrated by the introduction of *Garnisonsschulen* in Germany in 1692, the *Schulpflicht* of 1717 in Brandenburg/Prussia, and the office of the *Komisja Edukacji Narodowej* of 1773 in Poland, all of which led to radical educational reforms in the service of the state.

Despite the growth of supranational socio-economic structures, which also made the United Kingdom a member state of the European union, the dominant role of the nation state in education continues, confirmed by the heavy qualifications regarding harmonization of the education systems which surround collaboration in this domain by European union member states such as those contained in Article 126 of the Treaty on European Union. (For the full text of which see Appendix 2.)

In most countries teachers are counted as civil servants, entrusted that is, for example, according to the German definition, to 'act democratically and to impart a socialization as well as an education' to those in their charge in accordance with the constitution. The Weimar constitution of the German Reich spelled out the position in clearer terms than most:

The Reich, the states and the local authorities shall co-operate in their [the schools] organisation. The training of teachers shall be regulated in a uniform manner for the whole Reich, on the general lines laid down for higher education . . . Teachers in public schools have the rights and duties of state officials. (Article 143)

and:

All schools shall aim at inculcating moral character, a civic con-science, personal and vocational efficiency imbued with the spirit of German nationality and international goodwill. The duties of citizenship and technical eduction are subjects of instruction. (Article 148)

After the war the wording became somewhat more verbose, and it is necessary to look through a number of articles of the *Grundgesetz*, the Basic Law of the Federal Republic of Germany, to get the complete picture. Since this law was largely taken over from the Weimar constitution, however, together with rulings and regulations of the federal constitutional court affecting the civil service and the school curriculum, the position of education and the teachers in the state remains largely the same. Article 7 (para: 1) places the entire school system under state supervision, while Article 33 (para: 5) refers to the laws and regulations governing the professional civil service (Schmidt-Bleibtreu and Klein, 1973).

No other profession is given similar explicit mention in the German constitution, which shows how closely the responsibility for the issuing of certificates, such as the *Abitur*, the leaving certificate obtained after completing the selective secondary school (the *Gymnasium*), is identified with the state function of education. Though not normally counted by the general public among the German government bureaucracy, and in countries like Britain and Ireland not civil servants at all, teachers and their work are closely identified with the aims of education as determined by central authority and by the local authorities to whom they are responsible. In England and Wales it is the Secretary of State who according to *Education (Teachers') Regulations* 'must be satisfied' before qualified teacher status is granted (DES, 1984). A survey of the constitutions of other countries which refer to education, not all of them do so, reveals a similar position. The shock reaction to the newly acquired powers of the British Secretary of State in matters of education is due to their rather sudden emergence in such large numbers as a result of the 1988 Education Reform Act and subsequent legislation. What, in fact, is more disturbing is that, unlike mainland Europe, these powers are, in turn, delegated to a large number of unelected, nominated administrators in the form of 'quangos', that is 'quasi-autonomous non-governmental organizations'.

The analogies currently made between teaching hospitals and teaching schools for the professional development of teachers are revealed as false, since hospitals only cater for some sections of the population for some of the time as was pointed out by Anthony Adams in a letter to the *Times Educational Supplement* published on 8 July 1994. In Britain, unlike mainland Europe, education employers are perversely, in view of Government legislation, seen as separate from the state, and private industry was invited to comment on teacher preparation (DES, 1989).

Changing the Components of Teacher Education

Change in teacher education, with change in subject-teaching methods probably more overt than changes of content, happens for a variety of reasons. Though specific changes in the teaching methods used by teachers may only attract the attention of specialists, the pros and cons of different approaches to upbringing are discussed by the wider public. The interest created by the 'back to basics' movement in England and Wales formulated by the Prime Minister and the then Secretary of State for Education, on the occasion of the 109th Conservative Party Conference in October 1992, is an example. This is so, despite the fact that explicit public interest in education and upbringing, as opposed to professional or religious debate, is a relatively recent development associated with the growth of professional accountability to the public, accompanied by occasional outbursts against the professionals, voiced at the same conference.

Where change occurs it can be as fundamental and sweeping — approaches to child upbringing varying significantly from those advocates of unrestricted freedom, in 'the age of the child', to the belief in the total supremacy of the parent or educator over the child, including the right to inflict physical punishment (Stanley, 1992) — as discussion of subject content can be heated among specialists. Discussion of the latter has probably been more public in the case of the education of older age groups, while methods of teaching and upbringing are ostensibly felt more likely to affect younger children. Teacher education is involved in both cases.

In most countries, specific teaching methods in secondary education, recognized as such, appeared relatively late, long after they had been introduced into the syllabuses of elementary teacher-preparation courses. Method was regarded as superfluous if secondary teachers could go into a school teaching post straight after studying a subject, without receiving any preparation for teaching it. Partly because elementary education was traditionally perceived as affecting the whole person receiving instruction unlike the case of secondary schooling, which concerned the intellect only, training-course methods for the elementary sector were regarded as more complex. In Germany proportions of time allocated to courses in educational theory and general methods for future primary teachers are usually higher than those devoted to subject-teaching methods for those preparing for secondary schools.

In the timetables of elementary teacher-preparation courses there was relatively little time for the school subject (*Fach*) which had emerged from a university discipline (Aselmaier *et al.*, 1985). The total numbers of supervisors and the general impact of the work of a variety of supervising specialists may be less in evidence when teaching a subject to older pupils in secondary schools.

The Status and Professional Autonomy of Teachers

The fact that, in Prussia, training seminars for new grammar school (*Gymnasien*) teachers had been established some forty years (in 1787) before the first training (normal) schools for elementary teachers emerged, confirms the existence of another element in teacher education: that of 'status'. With greater importance attached to some forms of knowledge over others, allowing for differences of emphasis in different countries, the education of the older age groups and the preparation of subject, rather than class teachers, followed a path different from that of elementary school teachers.

The 'upbringing' part of schooling was seen as falling largely within the elementary teachers' concern. The introduction of teacher training for elementary teachers indicated the growing acknowledgment of the importance of their role in secondary socialization. The transfer of the responsibility for education to state or local authority was exemplified by the creation of state maintained schools. It contributed to enhancing the professional status of teachers and diminishing the roles played by parents, priests or other carers.

Change in teacher education is affected by change in the priorities in the requirements and expectations associated with education and upbringing and has at least as much to do with the professional efficiency of the teacher practitioners as it has with the socio-political climate of society at large, including government policies for teacher preparation. Only the domination of the free-market approach to education may explain the apparent discrepancy between putting an extra burden on the schools in England and Wales by locating most professional teacher preparation in them, although it is accepted (DES, 1991b) that they are falling behind in fulfilling their main task, which is that of educating children.

Changes in teacher-training courses thus reflect changes in the prestige and legitimacy accorded to certain forms of knowledge and skills as well as their utility to pupils; the latter can be taken as knowledge and skills useful to serve the various interests of the state. Designed by government officials, or in England and Wales parts of it by the then minister the school curriculum, for example, has exchanged virtually everywhere the teaching of classical languages for the teaching of the mother tongue. It has also increased the amount of time devoted to science and technology. The conservative New Democratic government in Greece twice reduced the role to be played by the demotic language in schools, the teaching of which had been placed there by the socialist PASOK party. The strong presence of *British* history after the latest proposals for the reform of the history curriculum in English schools (Dearing, 1994b) further confirms the point.

The teaching of moral and civic education is equally affected by the role of the state in education. In Britain the calls for a 'back to basics' curriculum have come from many brought up in a tradition of schooling which acknowledges the central role of the school in upbringing. The fact that in many countries of mainland Europe moral and religious education, including the area of religious instruction in schools, is left entirely to the churches which expect to look after their own faithful, highlights the distinctive role the secular school, as part of the state system, plays in moral, civic, and, indirectly, religious education in Britain.

Linked as it is with upbringing and secondary socialization, education is indeed a complex matter. In the UK, but especially in England, where, perhaps to a larger extent than in other countries in modern times, education has been identified with upbringing in all-day maintained and independent boarding schools, many curriculum policies and teaching approaches, including personal and social education (PSE), can be identified with religious and family values, in the teaching of which, until recently, the state has been less conspicuously involved. In view of the current distribution of powers it is well to remember that universal schooling provided by secular agencies in England did not begin until more than a century after provision in Prussia and Poland. In Scotland it was the churches who introduced comprehensive schooling as early as the sixteenth century.

This also accounts for the fact that, in Britain, the prestige of their educational practices is greater than the actual number of independent schools. Classroom approaches which attempt more than simple subject teaching and the inclusion of pupil–teacher and pupil–pupil relations, within the extra-curricular context of the school structure as a whole, to influence the learning and achievement processes of pupils as part of education have been singled out as a specifically English feature (Slee, 1991). The concept of the teacher acting *in loco parentis* is peculiar to Britain.

This helps to explain the complexity of teacher preparation in Britain which by including the inculcation of attitudes, through, for example, the development of courses in Personal and Social Education (PSE) courses, may involve more than the acquisition of subject-teaching methods alone. This factor has not figured amongst the reasons put forward for locating most of professional teacher preparation in schools.

The recent controversy surrounding moral and religious education in maintained schools in England, brought to the notice of the public by a letter in the *Guardian* in 1994 by the National Association of Head Teachers addressed to the Education Secretary himself, would meet with incomprehension in much of the rest of Europe.

Teacher Education and Europe

To improve general literacy and numeracy skills and knowledge essential for successful trading and manufacturing careers affecting the prosperity of the nation state changes are made in the school curriculum and in teacher education. This has certainly been an important factor in the overall increase of government influence on education in Britain which in turn has had an impact on teacher preparation.

In this respect educational change in Britain is paralleled by change in most of the rest of Europe as part of the aim to raise education standards in anticipation of improving the countries' socio-economic situation as member states of the European union. In the United Kingdom membership does not seem to be specifically invoked as a major impetus to the education changes introduced, however 'quality' education, the buzz word of conservative politicians, has included increased attention being paid to teaching modern foreign-language skills. Teacher education has a part to play in the entire process.

In keeping with the deliberate emphasis on more individualistic approaches to learning and upbringing and with the traditionally close school and family ties in education, current innovations in Britain can be seen as having been introduced in order to change pupils as personalities, to prepare them for entry into the competitive world of the free market economy to accentuate their individuality and to spur them on to achieving high levels of educational performance. Accentuating differences is one part of the consequences of the reforms. The introduction of national testing of pupils, the publication of school league tables, and the emphasis on competitive team games, little played in school time in mainland Europe, illustrate the concern with individual achievement. Direct preparation for 'Europe' is seen principally as preparation for an economic Europe which differs from the more cultural and international understanding priorities of recent educational reforms elsewhere, such as those in Portugal, with its growing network of European clubs in schools. In the United Kingdom 'Education for Citizenship' is little more than pupils' learning their consumer rights in a Citizens' Charter, with little regard to citizens' duties and obligations to fellow citizens, and even less reference to the community of citizens of Europe (Tulasiewicz, 1994). Scotland, which does not have to accept the educational changes introduced south of the border, appears more European in a number of respects when compared with England, an attitude supported by the Scottish General Teaching Council.

Where the social market sees schools principally as consumers, the position of teachers is bound to be affected. As William Halls noted some twenty years earlier teacher preparation takes heed of the prevalent out-look, which could be marked by primarily scientific, community or family concerns, or it can put the school leaver's future employment at the centre of educational activity. Within this brief, teachers may be called upon to act principally as purveyors of knowledge, counsellors, friends, moral tutors, or careers advisers. In the course of their dynamic relationship with pupils, parents, school governors and other members of society and authority at large they will be confronted by a number of new problems. Teacher-training institutions in Britain have had to keep pace with these developments, involving the introduction of the new issues, such as teaching courses about the creation of wealth; at the same time they have been helping to raise standards and to improve the social awareness of teachers in their professional preparation by the inclusion of topics such as intercultural education. This has often gone virtually unrecognized by a political establishment preoccupied with breaking with what it labels as 'left ideologies', a stance depending on government policies but less clearly marked in many other European countries.

Teacher Education: Reform and Ideology

In Britain educational change in the last fifteen years has been more of an ideological and *qualitative* change, with curriculum revisions not just those demanded in subject content by the Education Reform Act (DES, 1988) but, including also significant changes in the approach to upbringing in schools, such as the insistence on Christianity as the dominant religious tradition in the UK, while teaching other religions as are appropriate to the area in which the school is located. Reinterpretations of pupils' personal and social education, emphasizing moral education while making aspects of health education optional, can be cited to illustrate the upheaval. Changes in the structure of educational provision, such as the local management of schools (LMS) and encouraging schools to opt out of local authority control altogether and to apply for grant maintained (GM) status, which may be awarded by central government after a ballot by the parents, are indicative of a shift in two directions at once: increased populist control and increased state control.

In fact the aim is to create a new ideological basis for educating future Britons. The term 'quality' applied to education is used too loosely and too frequently, bereft of real meaning to inspire confidence that the new provision will indeed be more cost effective in economic and professional terms, a disquiet voiced by Her Majesty's Inspectors of Schools, teaching unions and individual teachers.

Current proposals for change in teacher education in England and Wales likewise represent an active, continuing process, envisage a radical transformation of present practice. Exhortations to concentrate on the teaching of subject matter to the virtual exclusion of a context in which subject lessons take place or the transfer of professional teacher preparation to schools cannot simply be interpreted as an attempt to improve teaching and teacher preparation, but are aimed rather to inculcate the new ideology by eliminating the intrusion of controversial political topics allegedly taught in higher education. In teacher education, in the words of Christopher Price, writing under the title, 'A new "vice anglais"' in the *Times Educational Supplement* (14 January 1994), this reduces teachers to technicians.

This trend lies behind attacks on educational theory in teacher training such as those emanating from the Centre for Policy Studies (Lawlor, 1990) and others, such as Anthony O'Hear (1988) which it is feared might introduce undesired discussion on such topics as the aims of education, differentiated schooling, or the link between pupil performance and social conditions. John Eggleston's warning in the *Times Educational Supplement* (3 September 1993) that 'educational studies are at risk' is perhaps too charitable when he simply notes that there is 'no script for the new teacher-training roles'. There clearly is a Conservative Party policy script.

In the 1987 run up to the general election Mr Dunn, the then junior education minister, said: 'We are choosing policies that any subsequent non-conservative government could not undo', words which spell out clearly the radical changes overall that are intended. The free-market ideology introduced by successive Conservative governments since 1979 has been convincingly identified by Ian Gilmour.

Contradictions and conflict may arise when these policies are applied, as when, for example, a pupil's Record of Achievement, produced by the teacher in consultation with the pupil, may give the child 'excellent' marks for effort which are not subsequently confirmed by marks achieved by him or her in formal nationally administered tests, an observation made by a senior Cambridgeshire teacher to the authors (1994).

Ministerial insistence on moving from assessment to testing continues to be opposed by public and professional opinion, seen for example, in the long drawn-out boycott of national testing particularly by the National Union of Teachers, to which few parents voiced objection. While such tests may be more reliable, in the sense of being self-consistent, they may not be as valid, in that they do not test relevant matters such as pupils' understanding.

Ideology, with its associated interpretations of history as well as of theories on child upbringing, then lies at the root of attempts to teach a new view of society and economic activity, exemplified by the former Prime Minister's (Lady Thatcher's) conviction that there is no such thing as society, or by her much criticized speech to the Scottish Kirk about there being a need for the rich in order to give alms to the poor.

The academic and personal education received by teachers before they embark on their professional preparation is bound to be affected by the changes. As the servants of the new order teachers will be expected to pass on its values to future generations. Particularly vulnerable is the status of teachers' professional preparation which, by concentrating on what are labelled as 'essentials' in terms of selective knowledge, approved skills, methods and morals, may exclude opportunities for the discussion of certain subject areas, such as wider concerns with society from the syllabus, mentioned above. This lessens the opportunity for independent thinking and reflection, for making comparisons and drawing conclusions, limiting teacher's preparation to 'observation' instead of 'experience'. It may be seen as an attempt to take away from teachers the dilemmas they now have to face, presenting them with certainties instead. Teacher education is too complex a topic to be reduced to subject matter alone without taking account of the pupils' personalities, their backgrounds, and the context of their subject teaching. In this context a dialogue between teachers and categories of employers on the subject of teacher preparation might uncover new content priorities.

Teaching is not the only profession currently faced with dilemmas in the exercise of their expertise. Doctors, for example, have to decide whether to operate on older people in view of the reduced availability of resources. However, teachers are faced with more dilemmas in their decisions, which affect more people, because they happen more frequently, and, once put into effect, may have more far-reaching consequences which are open to public scrutiny.

What Crisis in Teacher Education?

Crisis is our last point of consideration. This evocative word has often been heard in Britain when education is mentioned. The generous amount of space devoted to education in newspapers and magazines in England is used to draw readers' attention to the different priorities being canvassed and the changes and revisions that are constantly being introduced. The recent general extension in Germany of the period of teachers' professional preparation to two years and the gradual phasing in of West German practice in the preparation of teachers in the former GDR by sending many of them to train in what were the western *Länder* are small changes by comparison.

Crises occur when there is incompatibility between the different elements involved. For example, in the education system of a nation state, inadequate mathematics-teaching methods may be seen as putting the workers of that country at a disadvantage when seeking jobs, thus reducing its economic standing. In the same way, poor foreign-language teaching provision is often mentioned in education debates in the United Kingdom.

Crisis results when there is incompatibility between the structures of the education system maintained by the state and the views of the other agents involved such as those of the professional associations and teachers' trade unions. In England and Wales, for example, their published views on teacher education differ significantly from those exemplified by government policies. The unions do not support the concentration of all professional preparation in schools nor the total elimination of education theory from courses (NUT, 1993).

Crisis may also arise when incompatibility is the result of adopting a blatantly adversarial position in the process of introducing new policies, as is often the case in the United Kingdom. This differs markedly from the calmer tones of the debate surrounding the introduction of the *Instituts Universitaires de Formation des Maîtres* (IUFMs) in France (Ministère de l'éducation, 1993), despite its straddling two politically opposed administrations, and which included all interested parties including the unions. In England and Wales change in teacher preparation is presented so as to emphasize the split between opposing elements, for example between knowledge and practical experience, rather than seeing both as contributing parts to an integrated whole. Academic preparation, the study of the teaching subject as well as general education, is to be divorced from teachers' practical preparation, the latter provided almost exclusively by classroom teachers and located in a school. We would insist that it is the combined strength of the separate components named in the Introduction, which make up the holistic aspect of teacher preparation necessary to ensure high standards, vital in view of the long-term impact of teachers' responsibility for their pupils' lives.

Significantly different educational policies and practices, including the area of teacher preparation, being adopted in Britain from those of her European partners are a matter for concern. After the implementation in 1993 of the Single European Act and the Treaty on Union a 'less than European' system can leave Britain isolated and unable fully to cooperate with her partner states. Indeed, differences in the preparation of teachers might impair the smooth mutual recognition of teachers' qualifications throughout the European union impeding mobility and slowing down economic development.

Note

1 It may be helpful to emphasize that the education system in England and Wales forms a unity. That in Scotland is very different, as to, a lesser extent is that of Northern Ireland. The main concern in the following chapters is with changes in the educational system in England and Wales.

Chapter 2

Arriving at the Present Situation of Teacher Education in England and Wales

In spring 1994, the Conservative administration introduced into the House of Lords a new Education Bill which had two somewhat unconnected purposes. One was to introduce far-reaching reforms in the competences of the students' unions in higher education; the other was the establishment of a Teacher Training Agency (TTA) which would effectively transfer the financial base for teacher education from higher-education institutions to the schools.

The Bill, concerned with tertiary education, had a rough passage through the Lords, not unexpectedly given the large number of distinguished academics who sit in that House. The proposals for the Teacher Training Agency were amended, by a margin of three votes, to ensure that schools conducting their own programmes of teacher education would be required to do so in continued cooperation with higher-education institutions (HEIs). It is notable that the voices raised on this point were not simply divided along party lines. Amongst the Bill's opponents was, for example, the Conservative peer, Lord Beloff who said that the effect of the Bill would be to ensure that students in training schools would be taught by:

> people from the very generation whose political and educational philosophy is most challenged. They will be people who qualified, let us say, in the 1960s.

Whilst we would not accept for one moment the attack on the 1960s generation implicit here (a point to which we return later), the comment does show that, even judged by the Government's own arguments, there was something illogical about the Bill. The proposed changes in the rules governing the student unions had meanwhile been abandoned altogether.

In fact what really lay behind the Bill, as many speakers in the Lords, as reported in the *Times Educational Supplement* for 18 March 1994, pointed out, was an intention to obtain more power over the processes and content of teacher education which represented an ideological position. The Liberal Democrat Earl Russell (himself a distinguished university teacher) even went so far as to accuse the Government of imposing its own form of political correctness, saying that 'today's lunatic fringe is the day after tomorrow's orthodoxy', thus reminding us of the importance of keeping a variety of routes and approaches open rather than reducing them to a single alternative. When the Bill returned to the Commons the Government was determined to overthrow the Lords' amendment and to clear the way for the formal introduction of wholly school-based teacher training of the kind pioneered by a consortium of schools based in Bromley in Kent in 1993–4 and which was more widely introduced in the second half of 1994.

It is interesting to note that in July 1994, even though the Bill in its new form had not then been approved by the House of Commons, Geoffrey Parker, the former High Master of Manchester Grammar School (itself a well-known independent school), had already been appointed as chairman-designate of the proposed Teacher Training Agency, a post not due to be inaugurated until 1 September 1994. The main purpose of the Agency is to oversee the transfer of the funding for teacher education from higher education to schools which will be able to buy in expertise from HEIs if they wish to do so. The amount of funding involved here is considerable. According to DFE figures (DFE, 1993a) it amounts to £3,800 of government funding per student. The change of direction here had been made quite explicit: 'In future, the initiative . . . will come from those schools who choose to run their own courses' (DFE, 1993b). One of the effects of this was to bring initial teacher education much more firmly under ministerial control than ever before. In fact, even before the TTA had formally come into existence, the then Secretary of State for Education, John Patten demonstrated in a speech at Oxford, reported in *The Times* (9 July 1994) his determination to be interventionist in this respect. He opined that discredited teaching methods still championed on teacher-training courses were responsible for under-achievement by many children:

> Independent reports had found too much mixed ability teaching, not enough streaming of pupils, an over-reliance on topic work and insufficient focus on basics . . . Much of the fault lies in the stubborn refusal of some in teacher training to question the old orthodoxies and to embrace a different approach . . . The new Teacher Training Agency . . . would introduce more regular inspections and penalise departments where standards are low . . . What we cannot continue to ignore is the increasing evidence that assumptions made in the past about some methods of teaching have failed too many of our young people.

Not long after delivering this speech Patten was replaced in a Cabinet reshuffle by a new Secretary of State, Gillian Shephard, herself an ex-local education authority inspector. It remains to be seen whether she will adopt similar robust views to those of her predecessor and to what extent the chairman of the TTA will insist upon having things his own way. However, as so often in educational debate in this country, the real issues to do with the establishment of the TTA have failed to be discussed in rational terms and become merely a matter of party political adversary. As the *Times Educational Supplement* reported on 11 March 1994:

> The Labour Party has promised to scrap the new Teacher Training Agency if it wins the next general election . . . Critics say the new quango will represent an unwarranted increase in the Secretary of State's power, threaten academic freedom and drive a wedge between teacher training and the higher education system.

This promise was reiterated after the election of Tony Blair as the new leader of the Labour Party.

It remains to be seen what the real impact of the TTA will be but many in the schools, as well as HEIs, fear the worst. Writing in *Education* (15 July 1994), the journal that proclaims itself the voice of educational management, David Jamieson, Labour MP for Plymouth Devonport, maintained that:

> Even many of those schools the Government would like to consider as 'friends' were reluctant to stay on board. Harrow school pulled out of the scheme citing disruption of children's education as the reason. The AUT/NATFHE [the Association of University Teachers and the National Association of Teachers in Higher Education] confederation reported that, in the Birmingham area, 'all of the selected schools have now withdrawn from participation in partnerships, citing pressure on staffing structures and resources'. The schools are reported as saying the reasons for pulling out included, 'parental expectations that the pupils will have as much continuity of teaching from experienced practitioners as possible.'

In the same issue Fred Jarvis, a former general secretary of the National Union of Teachers (NUT), made the point that:

> while the Government is seeking an end to universal partnership between HE institutions and schools as a basis for teacher education in England and Wales it is busy promoting it in Scotland and Northern Ireland. Similarly, it has no plans for a quango [that is, the TTA] in those countries, or for Wales.

The Act establishing the new quango was only the latest in a series of Education Acts introduced from 1979 onwards, in the most radical set of changes in education since the 1944 Act, which represented a coordinated and planned programme of change at all levels of the education system, 'no longer a knee-jerk reaction', to quote a Minister of State in 1987, but a programme devised in such a way that it would be virtually impossible for successive governments to undo it.

From the middle of this period there was a series of changes in the system of teacher education which began by effectively taking away the autonomy of the HEIs in this respect by establishing the Council for the Accreditation of Teacher Education (CATE) in 1984. This body was essentially set up to impose programmes of teacher education to ensure that all courses leading to qualified teacher status conformed to criteria laid down by the Secretary of State for Education and Science (the details of these which appear in Appendix 2), the aim of which was to ensure an improvement in 'teaching quality' (DES, 1984).

According to the Government, this would best be done by locating teacher education in schools, a decision arrived at by constant appeals to 'quality', without any effective demonstration that there was any lack of quality in what was already happening. Indeed HMI conducted two surveys of the effects of initial teacher training, one in 1981 and one in 1987, both published under the title, *The New Teacher in School* (DES, 1982; DES, 1988). The later of the two reports, whilst not wholly uncritical, comments that:

> An encouraging feature of the 1987 survey is that the proportions of new teachers expressing satisfaction with a number of aspects of their training were higher than they were in the 1981 survey. In some aspects the improvement in the training, as indicated by the probationers' perception of how well prepared they felt themselves to be, was very marked. Such instances were in the preparation to teach children with different cultural backgrounds, for which the proportion feeling well trained, as opposed to merely adequately trained, increased from 29 per cent to 49 per cent between the two surveys, and in classroom management where the increase was from 49 per cent to 66 per cent. (DES, 1988)

Such an objective analysis as this, confirmed by later reports for example OFSTED (1993) does not appear to lend credibility to notions of complacency and 'out-datedness' on the part of the training agencies.

Following CATE, however, one-year postgraduate courses of teacher education for schools were extended to a mandatory thirty-six weeks, and the amount of time to be spent in schools gradually increased. By 1994 two-thirds of the time (that is twenty-four weeks) had to be spent in schools, and similar proportions of time applied to four year B.Ed programmes also.

There was no evidence from research, or any other source, that simply to extend the time spent in schools would do anything to improve 'quality'; it was seen simply as a 'common-sense' view advocated by ministers and 'obvious' to 'the man in the street'. At the same time there was a deliberate decision to ignore the other 'common-sense' view, expressed by HMI at the beginning of the debate (DES, 1991c) that:

> the prime purpose of schools, and the one to which governors and head teachers give priority, is to teach pupils, and not train students.

a view which seemed equally 'obvious' to many parents with children in the schools, and also to the governors who now had considerable legal responsibilities for ensuring the effective curriculum and management of schools.

This was a view shared also by the National Commission on Education, an independent inquiry into education, funded by the Paul Hamlyn Foundation, which arose from the presidential address of Sir Claus Moser to the British Association for the Advancement of Science in August 1990. He called there for a Royal Commission to be established to conduct:

> an overall review of the education and training scene: a review which would be visionary about the medium and long-term future facing our children and this country; treating the system in all its inter-connected parts; and, last but not least, considering the changes in our working and labour market scenes. (Walton, 1993)

Since, not unexpectedly, the request for a Royal Commission was immediately rejected by the Government, the British Association, together with other similar learned bodies, set up its own inquiry, the outcome of which, when published, generated considerable national interest in autumn 1993 (op.cit.). Its suggestions for the division of responsibilities in teacher education between HEIs and schools by no means support the proposals for an ever-increasing role for the schools. For example, HEIs are explicitly called upon to:

> develop knowledge and understanding in trainees, not just about teaching the national curriculum, but also about how children learn, about stimulating better ways of learning, about providing pastoral and careers guidance, and about assessment, management, equal opportunities and cultural awareness.

The schools, by contrast, are strongly urged to concentrate their energies very much on the practical, classroom elements of the training process.

What has already been written demonstrates the way in which the language of teacher education is constantly and subtly shifting, a point to which we shall frequently have occasion to return. In 1984, government-produced statements still refer to 'teacher education'; ten years later in 1994 the phrase had changed to 'teacher training'. This is more than a semantic point; it lies at the heart of a debate about how teachers are best prepared for the classroom that goes back well before the introduction of the changes just referred to. Further, no-one is likely to dispute the need to improve 'teaching quality'; it is the means whereby this is best achieved that is in dispute. At the present time the favourite word is partnership: teacher preparation is to be the outcome of a partnership between the teachers in schools and the lecturers and tutors in HEIs. However, under the present proposals, the 'partnership' is very much weighted in favour of the schools as the senior partners to the point where, now that the 1994 Bill has become law, HEIs may be excluded altogether.

The debate, in England, over how teachers are best prepared for their classroom roles has taken place ever since the formal training of teachers began in 1798 in a college in Southwark. From the beginning this was seen as a controversial matter. A group of admittedly 'radical left-wing lecturers' (their description of themselves), the Hillcole Group, characterized it thus:

> The college was considered a threat by the Church of England and the ruling elite who feared a challenge to their power from a literate working class. Not wishing to lose control of its grip on educational change, the Church decided to set up its own training colleges and by the middle of the 19th century had founded 20 institutions. The purpose of these colleges was to ensure that trainees would undergo a regime of 'instruction in facts' and in the 'training of character'. (Hillcole Paper 9, 1993)

Certificated teachers from these institutions would be employed in the church schools. The private (public) and the grammar schools which catered mainly for the children of the middle and upper classes were staffed generally by graduates from the universities, who had degrees in the subjects they taught and, with their personal and academic education complete, were not felt to need any further training.

The teachers in the elementary schools, established after the 1870 Education Act introduced compulsory elementary education for all, mainly acquired their classroom skills on the job transmitting a narrow range of knowledge and skills to their pupils, the brightest of whom often became teachers themselves learning on the job from their 'mentors' under the pupil–teacher system.

What we are witnessing under the legislation which has been introduced over the past ten years has tantalizing parallels with the brief history of teacher education which has been sketched above. Just as the Church-based teacher education colleges were established to ensure continuing control over the content of education and the moral health of the nation, so, in the present day, with a national decline in religious observance, education, according to Conservative Party guidelines, through control over entry into the teaching profession and through the National Curriculum, is seen as a means of ensuring the continuing moral well-being of the nation and its continuing sense of its own nationhood. The location of the bulk of initial teacher training in schools is a deliberate turning away from the HEIs, the training courses of which have been seen as ideologically tainted (Lawlor, op.cit.).

This has culminated in the development, spearheaded by a vocal and influential group on the Radical Right, of a call for a return to nineteenth-century values, including those enshrined in teacher preparation. This was all the more necessary since the conservative Right identified the '1960s' as the period of moral decline when pride in the nation diminished and the moral decadence of relativism in values began. Many of those working in teacher education in HEIs in the late 1970s and 1980s had held senior positions in schools in the 1960s; hence the need to protect young teachers from their influence and especially the 'trendy' methods of teaching they were claimed to have introduced under the influence of the Plowden Report, *Children and their Primary Schools*, of 1967 which explicitly recommended a balance of 'traditional' and 'progressive' teaching but which has consistently, in recent discussion, been characterized as only recommending the latter.

The headlong rush back to the past laid an emphasis on the view that all that a teacher requires is subject knowledge coupled with classroom skills which can be best learned on the job from a reasonably competent practitioner. But there was another purpose behind this also. In 1994, coming immediately after the somewhat reluctant signing by the Conservative administration of the Treaty of European Union, what had originally been seen as a necessary European economic union now became to be seen as a possibly dangerous threat to national sovereignty and identity. The insistence, in Article 126 of the Treaty, discussed in detail later (in Chapter 8), that there should be no harmonization of the educational systems of independent nation states and no establishment of a supra-national curriculum was endorsed by the Government.

The National Curriculum (a term not used for similar programmes of school study in other countries) told teachers what to teach and, through the establishment of a system of national testing, effectively how to teach it. The elaborate system of testing that resulted in which all pupils were supposed to be assessed on a basis of nationally applied tests at the ages of 7, 11, 14 and 16, was felt by most teachers to be a vastly increased burden taking up an inordinate amount of classroom time. As a result of considerable rebellion by classroom teachers, in 1994 for example only 10 per cent of maintained schools took the tests at age 14 and reported the results in English, mathematics and science.

Pressure from the schools led to the establishment of an inquiry under

Sir Ron Dearing which, reporting in December 1993 (Dearing, 1993), recommended a 'slimmed down' curriculum and a much simplified testing system to be introduced in September 1995 and intended to remain in place for at least five years.

The content of the curriculum as it emerged, both in its first manifestation and in its 'slimmed down' format, was essentially, especially in subjects such as history and English, unashamedly nationalistic, a 'nationalized curriculum' as it was called in the *Times Educational Supplement* of November, 1988. It was British history that was to be taught and English was to be based upon the dissemination of 'standard' (that is 'national') English and a canon of literary works in English that primarily celebrated traditional British values. The publication in 1993, quite exceptional in Britain, of a government-sponsored 'anthology' of prescribed texts to be read by all students in state secondary schools at the age of 13 is a pertinent illustration of this: it contained texts that largely celebrated a rural England of the past, far removed from the experience of most of the school pupils for whom it was intended. It went well with the evocation of the Prime Minister in one of his speeches about Europe where he insisted that, even after European union, England would remain a land of 'cricket, warm beer and maiden ladies cycling across country lanes on their way to church'.

This 'looking back' to a mythical and idyllic past is unique in Britain amongst the other countries of the European union where most concentrate upon the challenges of the twenty-first century, as has been well pointed out in an essay by Anne Corbett entitled, 'The Peculiarity of the English', included in *Education Answers Back*. (Chitty and Simon, 1993).

The implications of this, following hard upon the Act of European Union, are the subject of Part 3 of this book; here we are concerned primarily with its specific impact on teacher preparation in England and Wales. The 'quality' of which the UK Government speaks is essentially an 'old quality' based upon national feeling and upon knowledge of facts with an adherence to mystical Victorian values.

Effectively the debate that has been going on for well nigh twelve years has been over what knowledge is needed by teachers to enable them to do their job. It is characterized at one extreme by the view that all that teachers need is subject knowledge and classroom skills of exposition and control; at the other extreme is the view that teachers need a body of knowledge about educational theory as well.

It is the extreme views that have been predominant in Britain. Those who hold the first of these positions also generally hold the view that the National Curriculum should be as minimalist as possible, in practice a return to the nineteenth-century curriculum of elementary reading, writing and calculating. Those who hold the second position are themselves likely to be teachers of aspects of educational theory and therefore easily portrayed as seeking to further, or even retain, their own careers. (See, for example, Tulasiewicz *et al.*, 1992)

The debate really began with the publication of the James Report in 1972. Lord James, vice-chancellor of the University of Manchester, had been appointed to chair a committee of inquiry into the future of teacher education. In a collection of papers edited by Tyrell Burgess giving advice to the inquiry under the title *Dear Lord James* (Burgess, 1971) many of the authors stress the importance of classroom experience in teacher education. They charge that teacher education is 'academic and remote from reality'; however they also go on to make an important statement which remains true today:

> Up to a point, one would expect the training of teachers to be inappropriate for schools as they are. One of the purposes of teacher education is, after all, to change the practice of the schools. Many of the sneers from older teachers about the impracticability of training derive from nothing more serious than an instinctive defence of their own conservatism. (Burgess, 1971, p.10)

This still useful book, produced by the interestingly named Society for the Promotion of Educational Reform through Teacher Training, clearly shows that improvement in the schools (increased 'quality' in fact) will best be achieved through new approaches to teacher education. It argues, amongst other things, for 'main courses in children's language development' and 'new areas of study such as . . . environmental sciences or European studies . . . to meet the need of new courses being introduced in the more enlightened secondary schools', areas which only now are beginning to be included in many courses of teacher education.

Indeed what James principally reported in favour of was a greater integration of teacher education and in-service education. Initial teacher education (ITT) was to continue to take place in HEIs but was to be linked in the first years of teaching with an elaborate programme of in-service education for teaching (INSET) which would be compulsory for all new entrants into the profession. Part of this work would be done in the schools during the teachers' probationary period and part of it would be conducted in the HEIs to which the beginning teachers would return for the continuance of their training alongside their development of on-the-job classroom skills. Given the national pattern of teacher education and the fact that teachers might be recruited to areas where there was no effective HEI, the practicality of this was not immediately apparent and the James Report was never implemented, although, in Scotland, the probationary period of two years operates alongside the in-service courses run in the training institutions. This extended probation period is also a feature of most other member states of the European union.

What the James Report did do, however, of lasting importance was to confirm the notion of partnership between schools and HEIs, to stress the importance of INSET throughout a teaching career, and to open up the debate about the relevance of educational theory to the development of teachers. James' notion of partnership was a much more equitable one than that which is, if at all, envisaged under present proposals. Under contracting funding and the local management of schools (LMS) organized INSET linked with the HEIs is now virtually extinct. Educational theory is fundamentally under attack, especially by Conservative politicians basing their views on those of the Centre for Policy Studies, the independent right-wing think tank which has exerted an influence on government quite unrelated to its numbers and the fact that it is a totally self-appointed group.

It is hardly surprising that James is little referred to in the present debate. Nonetheless his Report is really where the recent history of teacher education in England and Wales in the 1970s begins and at the time it led to a major debate in the HEIs. This debate tended to focus around the issue of the future of educational theory, or what began increasingly to be called educational studies and their relation to the teaching of subjects, 'methods' studies. In many HEIs, including the Department of Education in the University of Cambridge, there were attempts to develop courses that linked the two kinds of studies together and sought also to link more whole-heartedly with the work going on in schools (see the essay by Walford and Raffan in Alexander and Whittaker, 1980 and Tulasiewicz, 1986). The move towards an increased emphasis upon practicality in teacher education was well under way.

The debate over the future direction of teacher education led to a conference on the future of the Post Graduate Certificate of Education (PGCE), organized by the University Council for Education in Teaching (UCET) held at King's College, London in autumn 1975, chaired by Paul Hirst, then professor of education at Cambridge. Hirst's specialism and academic reputation was based upon his work as a philosopher of education. It came as something of a surprise to many, therefore, how firmly he embraced the new doctrine of practical, classroom-based work at the expense of educational theory. In his opening address to the conference (Hirst, 1976) he made his newly espoused position quite apparent:

> Most professional trainers of teachers do in fact now seem to reject the idea that the PGCE course should be explicitly concerned with liberal education. There is, however, evidence . . . of a much greater reluctance to reject the aim of a study of the nature of education, its institutions and their history, beyond the demands of direct training for teaching . . . There are vast areas of educational psychology, educational administration, sociology, philosophy, history of education, comparative education, and even curriculum theory which have no really justifiable place in a PGCE course. We need to filter out the elements in these areas that are in fact significant for the practical business of teaching and to

restrict ourselves to these . . . To move a stage further by limiting the aims of the course to preparing students for their first teaching jobs would surely be an added note of realism in our planning. (Hirst, 1976)

By no means everyone agreed with Hirst in this respect and his view was characterized by some as a kind of 'narrow practicism', though he himself was to describe it later as a 'theory in practice' approach, an aim of which was, echoing Schön (1983) to produce the 'reflective practitioner'. Indeed, Hirst himself has returned to a somewhat modified view on this in later publications (Hirst, 1990).

However, at the same conference the contrary view was firmly urged by Professor Brian Simon of the University of Leicester who accused Hirst of precisely that narrow practicism which he traced, rightly, to the influence of the James Report (Simon, 1976):

This paper is concerned to argue the importance of maintaining and strengthening the theoretical aspects of the PGCE course . . . Consideration of these matters is both urgent and appropriate in view of the pressures now being exerted to confine the PGCE course purely to the preparation (or 'training') of the student for competence in his first job in the classroom. Reduction of teacher education to this 'practicist' objective derives initially from the report of the James Committee, which was sceptical of the value of educational theory and which, in any case, placed great emphasis in the professional preparation of the teacher on its proposals for the induction (or probationary) year and on inservice release for all teachers . . . The PGCE year should emphasize preparation of the student for his role as a class teacher, but should also give some emphasis to his preparation as a member of a profession. (Simon, 1976)

The rest of the conference became essentially a discussion of these two contrasting positions. It is noteworthy that in Simon's contribution quoted above an opposition is suggested between teacher 'education' and teacher 'training', a word used here in a clearly pejorative sense, and also that a further paper (Lacey and Lamont, 1976) was devoted to the issue of 'Partnership with Schools', an increasing vital issue for the 1990s, to which we return in Chapter 4.

The language of the debate was beginning to be firmly established and would move shortly in the 1990s into the currency of the marketplace.

Chapter 3

The Rhetoric of Teacher Education

Every time the question of language surfaces, in one way or another, it means that a series of other problems are coming to the fore: the formation and enlargement of the governing class, the need to establish more intimate and secure relationships between the governing groups and the national-popular mass, in other words to reorganize the cultural hegemony.

Antonio Gramsci

The previous chapter has already indicated that the changes proposed to teacher education have been reflected by shifts in the way the language concerned with teacher education is used, in fact that a new rhetoric of teacher education is being constructed. It is the purpose of this chapter to examine these changes in some detail and to show that, at the heart of the manipulation of the language, lies a fundamental regrouping of power whereby the 'governing groups' seek to forge a union with the 'national-popular mass'.

In the consumerist society that has been the hallmark of the United Kingdom since the mid-1980s, education has itself become a market commodity, with an implicit competition between the stall-holders in the market-place for the selling of their products. We have seen the trumpeting of parent power, such as the opening up of school places to free parental choice, embodied in the 1993 Education Act. On 27 February 1993, John Patten speaking to the Conservative Local Government Conference opined that as a consequence of these policies: 'certainly popular schools would expand and poor schools would close'. This presents a false dichotomy, stressed here by the alliteration between 'popular' and 'poor', since 'popular' does not necessarily mean 'good', and ignoring the issue of the number of pupils who have to be found places where no 'popular' schools may exist.

Such market competition could be escalated to the point of combativeness as was shown in the Prime Minister's, John Major's, speech to the same conference when he stated that:

the left would be defeated on the battlefield of education by a Conservative Party that had thrown away the 'nostrums' of the 1960s. (John Major)

Mr Major's use of the deliberately obscurantist word 'nostrums' damns all the educational programmes and policies of the 1960s as if they were cheap patent medicines, whilst the sound of the word has overtones of 'tantrums', associated with unruly children, who can be corrected by the good dominie.

A further instance, already hinted at in the previous chapter, of the use of rhetoric to achieve a quick sale can be seen in the appeal to marketability, in the use of the word 'quality', in a totally undefined sense, so as to make the product ('education') more attractive to the customer. It is a circular argument since no-one is likely to argue for a diminution of quality either in the schools or in teacher education. We are concerned here with particular reference to teacher education, to draw attention to the dangers of the political manipulation of language to serve particular ideologies, by identifying some of the ways in which this can be achieved.

It is not, of course, a new phenomenon. George Orwell, writing in *Politics and the English Language* (Orwell, 1946) put it like this:

> Political language . . . is designed to make lies sound truthful and murder respectable, and to give an appearance of solidity to pure wind. (Orwell, 1946)

and went on to warn us that:

> One cannot change all of this in a moment, but one can at least change one's own habits, and from time to time one can even send . . . some worn-out and useless phrase . . . into the dustbin where it belongs. (Orwell, op.cit.)

Another example of this kind of manipulation of language, used to make the proposed political policies acceptable, is given by the American researcher, Claire Lerman, working in Cambridge in the early 1970s, on the language used by successfully campaigning politicians, who coined the useful notion of the Institutional Voice (IV):

> The Institutional Voice does not speak in its own personal capacity, but equates itself with its office or role, rather like the royal 'we'. It identifies its policies with 'the good of all', 'national security', 'public interest', 'our way of life', and so forth. It alone has the right to speak for the nation or institution; it is the repository of power and tradition; and it makes a unique claim to virtue . . . [It] accomplishes this by transforming the topics of discourse. (Lerman, quoted in Chilton and Aubrey, 1983)

Lerman suggests that, to do this, the Institutional Voice employs certain powerful linguistic and rhetorical devices. In listing these we can associate them with some of the language used to talk about both education and, in particular, teacher education. Thus the IV uses:

1   the choice of grammatical constructions that avoid explicit reference to cause, agents, time and place
    For example, a Higher Education Funding Council circular, dated November 1992, spoke of the need for the 'Recognition of Excellent Quality Education on ITT courses' with no reference to the agencies whereby the undefined 'excellent quality education' in initial training might be achieved.

2   the preference for, and production of, particular words and metaphors, hiding some aspects of a reality and heightening others
    Here we might immediately think of such phrases as 'the economics of the market-place', 'the delivery of the curriculum', and the notions of 'choice' and 'user's rights'.

3   the invitation to draw inferences as a consequence of the above so as to evoke wider patterns of unspoken belief
    This may be seen in populist notions such as the appeal to 'common sense' and the identification of basic ills (such as is manifest in the demonization of the 1960s) and in instant remedies, such as the transfer of teacher training to schools.

An early application of this to the present debate about teacher education may be seen in the fact that the White Paper (DES, 1983) was entitled '*Teaching* Quality', not '*Teacher* Quality' [our emphasis]. The use of the abstract noun 'teaching' (instead of the personalized use of 'teacher') effectively removes the sense of the human operator who alone can be responsible for improving quality. This can be seen as part of a systematic process of eliminating the professional presence of teachers, or, at least, undermining their status in the eyes of the general public. In the title we note, too, the beginnings of an attempt to capture the moral and economic high ground by the use of the 'trigger' word: quality.

There has, therefore, been brought together, in the last few years, an assault upon the teaching profession alongside that on teacher educators. In the name of the Office for Standards of Education (OFSTED) we see the same process continuing. OFSTED, established in 1992, has largely replaced Her Majesty's Inspectorate as a new 'independent' Inspectorate and the word 'standards' (similar in its use to 'quality') is easily linked with proposals for performance-related pay to bring about a compliant, as well as an efficient, workforce.

It may be here that we can identify the elusive link between the two parts of the 1994 Education Bill. The establishment of the Teacher Training Agency was linked in the Bill with the intended destruction of the power of the student unions and with the removal of the status of 'students' from prospective teachers, replacing that term by the increasingly used term, 'trainee'. The use of this term seems to us to lower the status of students and their ability to behave as autonomous beings. It places an emphasis upon an undue reliance on classroom 'skills and performance'. (These have now been defined in terms of 'competences' which are addressed in Appendix 2), the establishment of the *effective* practitioner as a replacement for the *reflective* practitioner that had been argued for in earlier years (Schön, 1983). In similar terms, the Government prefers to eschew the word 'professionalism', one which it always uses in a derogatory sense, insisting instead upon the primacy of 'common sense' and 'basics'. Indeed the then Secretary of State is on record of saying about primary education (in the *Guardian*, 19 January 1993) that more whole-class teaching and the reintroduction of lessons based upon specific subjects simply represents 'a return to plain old-fashioned common sense'.

Another of the Government's relatively recent interventions in teacher education can be seen in the issue of Circular 9/92 (DES, 1992) on 'Initial Teacher Training (Secondary Phase)' which set out the major pattern for courses of training to be in place in all HEIs by September 1994. This was later followed by 'A Note of Guidance from the Council for the Accreditation of Teacher Education' (CATE, 1992), popularly known as CATE 3. This was, in fact, CATE's swan-song as it was abolished and replaced by the Teacher Training Agency on 1 September 1994.

Here the pattern of rhetoric continues. Circular 9/92 provides the first sign of the new financial arrangements that are to be introduced. It indicates that:

> the Government intends that the increased contribution of partner schools to teacher training should be recognized, through transfer of resources from HEIs

Here the Government evades its responsibilities of considering the cost implications of this by subtly going on to say that:

> transfers should . . . be negotiated locally . . . [and] the Secretary of State does not intend to intervene in the event of disagreements . . . between HEIs and individual schools, but the costs to schools and the resources transferred will be monitored closely

The bland official sounding language conceals implicit threats of what will happen if institutions do not do as they are told. Already many HEIs are making contingency plans which would make it possible for them to lay off staff to enable this 'transfer of funding' to take place. More seriously still, it has recently become clear that a number of HEIs are considering leaving initial teacher education altogether. For example, it was announced in the *Observer* that:

London's University of the South Bank has axed a course training teachers in subjects such as maths and modern languages, in which there is a [teaching] staff shortage. Up to 70 graduates will have to seek places elsewhere. (The *Observer*, 15 May 1994)

At the same time the chairman of the Committee of Vice-Chancellors and Principals (CVCP), Keith Edwards of Leicester University, warned that:

Some colleges are pulling out and others are reconsidering. There will come a point when we will have to decide whether we can afford to continue with teacher training.

The problem here is one that we have already noted elsewhere: once the infrastructure has been destroyed it will take a considerable time to build it up again. The wholesale transfer of teacher education to schools may become a reality, not because anyone (except a few ideologues) really wishes it to happen but because a process has begun which will, in a short time, become virtually unstoppable. Even the schools are becoming increasingly concerned and weighing in on behalf of the HEIs. For example, in the same *Observer* article, the headteacher of a school in Kettering is quoted as saying that:

It will become increasingly difficult to find schools prepared to take students. Many schools have become very money-conscious. A few schools will take more and more students and that will mean complaints from parents. *Most worrying of all is the prospect of universities pulling out altogether.* [our emphasis]

The potentially laudable notion of 'partner schools', first appearing in this sense in Circular 9/92, is glossed in CATE 3 which stated that 'HEIs and schools should form partnerships to ensure an effective school-basis for training'. Of the paper's nineteen pages, nine are devoted to a fuller examination of the meaning of partnership. From these, it is clear that, in the detailed arrangements, the schools will have 'a leading responsibility' for the professional development of students while the role of the HEIs will be reduced to responsibility for teaching subject studies ('where required') and for 'validation and accreditation requirements'. In addition they will, in having the responsibility for 'arranging student placements', be effectively reduced to something more like the status of a booking office than that of an HEI, since it is clear from 9/92 that HEIs will not even have a free choice of the schools they use:

Where HEIs do not accept a school's offer of partnership, they should make clear the reason for their decision. The Secretary of State reserves the right to withhold approval from . . . courses of

initial teacher training if there were evidence that individual schools
had been treated arbitrarily or unreasonably.

The use of these emotional appeals to fairness ('unreasonably', 'arbitrarily') reveals the Government's desire to influence an appeal to the 'ordinary voter', whose own experience will generally be far more likely to
encompass schools than HEIs. In fact it has become clear that what lies
behind the language (and its lightly veiled threats) is a determination that
HEIs shall be compelled to train their students in independent schools,
Grant Maintained Schools, and City Technology Colleges, all favourite
projects of the Government and its advisers.
    There is a further requirement in 9/92 that:

> HEIs should make explicit . . . to schools their criteria for the for-
> mation of partnerships . . . [including] the use of indicators as evid-
> ence of quality and learning.

This has the effect of giving a legalistic and commercial language to this
process, which cannot work since, in practice, no real commercial partnership could ever come into existence, or survive, on such unequal terms.
The 'market-place' interference with what is essentially a matter of professional judgment is highlighted by the fact that, in Germany, the civil
service can produce a similar arrangement on an almost collegiate basis,
allowing the student, for example, a choice of 'mentors', without the need
for any kind of legalistic documents such as the 'contracts' now, in many
cases, being drawn up between the schools and the HEIs on a purely
mercantile basis.
    In the final stages of this debate other terms have been slipped into
everyday parlance alongside that of 'partnership' and 'training', for 'education', and 'trainee', for 'student'. The supervising teacher in the schools
has become a 'mentor', an unfortunate metaphor since it tends to entail
seeing the mentor as more like the 'craft master' of old who usually
produced replicas of himself rather than independent and reflective
practitioners.
    The word 'mentor' itself has an interesting history as we are reminded
in Caldwell and Carter (1993), *The Return of the Mentor*. This timely study
is concerned with 'workplace' mentoring in a variety of contexts, in health
and industry, as well as education. In this work, an article by Carruthers
points out that the original Mentor was, in Greek mythology, left to look
after Odysseus' son, Telemachus, while his father went to fight the Trojan
Wars. He comments that, this being so, Mentor had to be:

> a father figure, a teacher, a role model, an approachable counsel-
> lor, a trusted adviser, a challenger, an encourager, among other
> things, to the young Telemachus in order that he become, in time,

a wise and good ruler. . . . [He] was admirably endowed to oversee the growth of Telemachus from innocent boyhood to splendid
manhood. (Caldwell and Carter, 1993)

While we may doubt whether the present generation of teacher-mentors
can match these qualities it is also interesting that the examples that Caldwell
and Carter cite in their study of mentoring in teaching are primarily concerned with *peer* mentoring, far removed from the apprenticeship role that
the trainees are currently assuming in the schools.

In terms of teacher education the term 'mentor' has appeared recently
and swept the board without any clearly defined or agreed definition of
the duties or responsibilities of those so called. There are several ways of
looking at this. One, minimal mentoring, is no more than the provision
by experienced teachers of support through their own practice to the new
teacher. This can be done in a teaching-practice school where the mentors
carry out their normal teaching duties but, in doing so, they are observed
by beginning teachers. A second form of mentoring employs a more
distinctive way of helping new teachers learn how to teach. In this case
established teachers have supervisory duties and become responsible for
devising enabling strategies to be learned, used and tested by the new
teacher as discussed in McIntyre, Hagger and Wilkin (1993). A yet more
developed model of mentoring may include collaborative teaching, involving joint planning, with the new teacher only undertaking certain
tasks in the classroom. The mentor's experience and knowledge are placed
at the new teacher's disposal as are the full resources of the school. This
provision of a framework of support may continue long after classroom
competence has been achieved.

The current use of the term in England has tended to exclude some
of these positive aspects of mentoring and has become assumed to imply
more of a client-like model. On the whole, too, little thought has been
given to the training and time needed for a mentor to operate effectively.
In the practice of many other countries, such as both Germany and the
USA, mentoring has been undertaken through a close partnership between the mentors in schools and their colleagues in higher education
along the lines we describe in Chapter 7.

With the advent of the Teacher Training Agency the final pattern for
the virtually wholesale destruction of the role of higher education in teacher
education has been completed and the task of the practical education of the
new teacher has been transferred wholly to the schools, whether or not
they are prepared or equipped to undertake this responsibility.

We have seen in this chapter, through a careful analysis of the rhetoric
that dominates the relevant documents, that present policies are entirely
conserving ones intended to make 'the consumer' look back to pre-1960
'quality', and to stop any innovations except those agreed upon by the
Government, or, more accurately, its small group of largely self-appointed,

and generally unelected advisers, accountable to shareholders' meetings, at which the ordinary shareholder is rarely to be seen, 'the Guardians', in Plato's sense of the term, of the system.

The dangers of this approach have been robustly characterized in an address given in July 1992 by Eric Bolton, a former senior chief inspector of schools (reprinted in Chitty and Simon, 1993).

His words, in the delightfully entitled chapter, 'Imaginary Gardens with Real Toads', are worth quoting here at some length:

> Without some underpinning theory . . . a public education service simply limps from one bureaucratic decision to another, or conversely, lurches around maniacally, subject to the whims and passions of self-interest and to the rantings of whichever fashionable voices are currently able to gain access to influential ears.
>
> Sadly, despite the rhetoric of Citizen's and Parent's Charters, the Government shows little sign of being a listening Government.
>
> When it does, it listens so selectively that most of those in the education service fear that what they have to say falls on deaf ears. The Government does not seem to listen to:
> 1 Heads and teachers; teacher associations; governors and education researchers, on the difficult issues of school effectiveness, value-added and league tables. It *does* listen to John Marks and the Adam Smith Institute.
> 2 Heads of schools; governing bodies; head teacher associations; vice-chancellors and teacher trainers, when it sets out to reform teacher training. It *does* listen to Sheila Lawlor whose critique of Initial Teacher Training is based on a somewhat selective reading of course prospectuses and is not complicated by ever having visited and systematically observed what goes on.
> 3 Public examination boards; chief examiners; most heads and teachers; HMI and large employers, when it sets to squeeze the GCSE back into a GCE 'O' level mould. It *does* listen to the Centre for Policy Studies and a small group of independent school heads. (Bolton in Chitty and Simon, 1993)

In short, the rhetoric is in itself a matter of concern, but what is a matter of much greater concern are the consequences to which it has led in a few short years and which, in their turn, prompted the occasion for this book.

Chapter 4

Many Routes: One Destination

The Various Routes

Until relatively recently the way into teaching in England and Wales was clear-cut. Basically one either took a degree, in a discipline usually, though by no means always, related to the subject one intended to teach, followed by a one year Post Graduate Certificate of Education course, in the same or another university or college (the consecutive model), or one studied for three or four years, usually the latter, engaged on a Bachelor of Education (BEd) degree course (the concurrent model), also including the academic study of one or more subjects, normally related to the subjects or age range one intended to teach.

Both routes included elements of educational studies (often called foundation studies). These would, in more recent years, have been such areas as philosophy, sociology and psychology of education. In earlier times they would also have included the possibility of studying both the history of education and comparative education. Though the latter two fields of study have fallen from fashion, from the perspective of this book we feel that they have an especial value. In particular, the study of sociology has been strongly criticized by those arguing for the 'reform' of teacher education as being ideologically biased towards 'the left', even though it is difficult to assign any evidence to support this view. These studies were supplemented by a further area of study, that of how to teach one or more subjects in the classroom ('methods studies'), together with practical classroom experience ('teaching practice'). For the sake of clarity, we use in this chapter the terms that have traditionally been used in education courses. Elsewhere in the book, especially in Part 3, we suggest a new model for teacher education in which we propose a slightly different terminology.

There was, in addition, a further route, though one pursued by many fewer students, and only available in a few universities, such as Cambridge, York and Aberystwyth, a BA which included a substantial element of educational studies in the undergraduate programme alongside one or more other subjects. This, too, was generally followed by a PGCE which provided the necessary practical experience through teaching practice. Thus, almost invariably, the aspirant teacher would undertake a four-year study programme followed, until 1993, by a one-year probationary period, and supplemented throughout a teaching career by part or full time in-service education, which might include study for higher degrees or diplomas in the field of education. In Scotland the course lasted for five years, a four-year degree course followed by a one-year PGCE course, undertaken in a College of Education, emphasizing the professional component of preparation for teaching and still followed by a two-year probationary period.

This relatively simple structure has now been superseded by a bewildering variety of routes, described in some detail in Barrett *et al.* (1992). These included the articled and licensed teachers schemes. The first of these was introduced in 1990 for both primary and secondary teachers and enabled graduates without any teaching qualifications to enrol in a two-year course of training, 80 per cent of which took place in schools. The successful completion of the course led to the award of a PGCE. The scheme, originally designed to meet teacher shortages in certain subjects, has been highly controversial and not adjudged a success and it is being phased out. From September 1993 it has only been available for intending primary teachers. The licensed teachers scheme, also introduced in 1990, involves prospective teachers who have had at least two years of higher education related to their intended teaching subject. They must also be at least 24 years old and they are appointed directly to posts in schools. They receive individual training while in post for two years. After successful completion of this, they receive qualified teacher status (QTS). Those following the licensed teachers route need not necessarily be graduates. The scheme is used meanwhile predominantly for prospective teachers arriving from the Republic of Ireland.

Galvin (1994) points out:

the licensing experiment has been marked by a significant absence of research that documents and evaluates the scheme; both of the major reports commissioned to this end by the government have seen misadventure. The HMI report . . . was disappointingly vague . . . But it was at least published: the NFER [National Foundation for Educational Research] report was not. So it has fallen to a relatively subsidiary component of the Modes of Teacher Education Project (MOTE) — published as Barrett and Galvin (1993) to supply the bulk of publicly available data on practice and provision across the scheme nationally. (Galvin, 1994)

He concludes:

The cardinal significance of research into the licensed teacher scheme is that it illustrates at the very least the questionable nature of recent hasty moves towards school-centred initial teacher training. Even within the relatively small-scale numbers of the licensing scheme, few schools were found to be capable of offering high-quality ITT or had the infrastructure in place to do so . . . In addition the training and on-site support of mentors was wholly inadequate for the task they were being asked to undertake. In short, the keystones of the licensing scheme were missing or fundamentally flawed. (op.cit.)

These innovations represented a first attempt by the Government to re-form the traditional patterns of teacher education and to move away from what had by now become an all-graduate profession. Alongside them, the traditional routes, already described, have remained in place, though as we have already seen, they are very much under threat.

In particular, government policies announced in a Circular 14/93 (DFE, 1993) indicate that the BEd is likely to be reduced to a three-year period as the norm, rather than the four years that have become more or less universal at present. This is likely to have the effect that many HEIs, which currently offer a four-year Honours BEd course, will withdraw from this area of work altogether rather than countenance the inevitable diminution in academic standards that will result from the shorter period of study.

The Government Proposals

It is worth quoting the main proposals of the draft circular since they well represent the reasons that underlie current government thinking. They envisage:

- tough new criteria which all training courses must meet, focusing on the subject knowledge and teaching skills new teachers require to be effective in the classroom;
- a greater role for schools, which are best placed to help student teachers develop and apply practical teaching skills;
- a continuing need for study in higher-education institutions of the subject knowledge necessary for sound teaching of the National Curriculum;
- a greater diversity of courses, including in particular:
  — a new three-year, six-subject BEd to prepare teachers for work across the primary curriculum;
  — a new one-year course for those with experience of working with children, preparing them to teach nursery and infant pupils;
  — courses preparing teachers for work as subject specialists at Key Stage 2 [that is age 11, the final years of primary schooling].

The most controversial element of these proposals, the one-year course for 'those with experience of working with children', became known derisively as the recruiting of a 'Mum's Army', and was subsequently withdrawn. It does, however, indicate the extraordinary assumption of the Government and its advisers that little 'training', or indeed knowledge, is needed in order to teach very young children. This cynical contempt for the early stages of learning sits badly with the desire to then introduce 'subject specialists' at Key Stage 2. Subject knowledge, as defined by the relatively narrow confines of the National Curriculum, becomes all important; education in broader, more liberal terms does not.

The purpose of this chapter is to consider some of the principles that lie behind these varying routes and to argue the case for the retention of the best elements of traditional and well-proven routes into teaching.

Apart from the ideological considerations discussed in previous chapters, the reasons for the changes that are being introduced can be summed up under five headings: academic knowledge, professional preparation and location. In the current British context, the other two, cost and control, assume significance unparalleled in other European Community member states.

The most contentious issue is the extent to which teacher education (or training) should be located in higher-education institutions or in the schools. Two other considerations follow from this. If it is the school where the training is to be located, the cost of training will have to be transferred from the HEIs to the schools, something that has, of course, important implications for staffing in both institutions. Further, if the bulk of the training is to be carried out in the school, the school rather than the HEI will increase more and more its control of the content of that training: an apprenticeship model is likely to replace a professional model for the work.

This, in its turn, will have important implications for the assessment of students and the means whereby that assessment is to be validated. Increasingly, with the talk of 'competences' and 'performance indicators', the individual is subordinated to the cause of efficiency. The very language shows how the philosophy of the market triumphs so that both education and teacher education lose contact with their liberal humanistic roots, a point to which we return in Part 3.

The process of assessment will also differ according to the rigour that schools bring to bear upon it. The way for this has already been paved by the abolition in England and Wales of the probationary year so that there is now no formal 'rite of passage', or induction, into the profession of teaching. It is difficult to evaluate the success of the different schemes for entry into teaching which exist at present though some work towards this has been done by the Modes of Teacher Education (MoTE) project, a collaborative research project involving researchers from five HEIs and funded by the Economic and Social Research Council (ESRC). It is expected that its main publication will emerge at the end of the project, probably around January 1996 though some of its preliminary findings are available in Whitty *et al.* (1992). Significantly, the Government has de-creed an expansion of the totally school-based route in 1994–5 even before the first year's experiment was completed, much less evaluated.

As we show in Part 2, these developments put us out of step with most of our partners in the European union and not only there. New patterns of teacher education are indeed needed for a change in Europe but they should be both forward looking, built upon a thorough assessment of the situation and the new needs. The fundamental argument against the various forms of school-based training is that they are limiting. The school-based trainers are likely to have experience and direct knowledge of a narrow range of schools; they are likely to seek to replicate in the next generation of teachers only those models of teaching with which they have themselves achieved success.

The situation is that the challenge of change is at present imperative. Not only are there the opportunities afforded by the European Union, there is the introduction at an ever-increasing pace of the new technologies into the classroom with a consequent 'de-skilling' of many established teachers, and there is the pressure for the introduction of new subjects in the curriculum in a multicultural Europe, such as environmental studies, European studies and tourism.

The essentially market-led nature of whole school-based training links directly with the conservative nature of the National Curriculum and the market-place economy of handing money directly to the schools to spend under the policies of Local Management of Schools (LMS), and also with the erosion of the power of the Local Education Authorities (LEAs), which incidentally used to be the gate-keepers into the profession since they had responsibility for passing or failing the new entrants' probationary year.

It has been noted by some commentators that it may not be a coin-cidence that the proposals for the transfer of the funding of ITT to the schools come at the same time as the formulation of plans to require undergraduate students to finance part of their university fees out of their own pockets. It would be difficult to justify this if postgraduate courses for teaching were to continue to be exempt from students paying their own fees. However to introduce student fees for prospective teachers would not only be deeply unpopular but would seriously deter recruitment. The policy of establishing the Teacher Training Agency with the money, and therefore the controlling power, passing away from HEIs, may well have been influenced by these purely fiscal, rather than educational, concerns. Unlike North America, salaries in Britain are unlikely to entice students to embark on a teaching career in large numbers and shortages still exist in some subjects such as physical science and mathematics.

It is notable that all of this applies solely to England and Wales. In Scotland there remains a two-year probationary period; the HEIs still have a strong controlling interest in teacher education, extending increasingly into the probationary years when students will continue to follow some courses in the HEIs; and the LEAs still have considerable authority and influence. There is also a powerful gate-keeper in the shape of the General Teaching Council (GTC).

Thus totally, or even largely, school-based courses would not pass muster in Scotland. Teachers who have been trained south of the Border, if they wish to teach in Scotland, will be required to undergo a two-year probationary period and may be required to take extra courses provided by the HEIs before they attain full recognition by the GTC.

Recruitment of New Entrants

The decision was made by the Department for Education (DFE) to encourage mature entrants into the profession by funding, to the extent of £2.3 million, a new part-time Open University (OU) PGCE. This is for both primary and secondary teachers, the latter, to begin with, in six subject areas: English, mathematics, science, technology, history, and French, with an initial plan to train 1,000 students a year divided equally between the primary and secondary sectors. When the project was announced in August 1991 it received over 10,000 enquiries from prospective students indicating that there was a genuine need for such provision at the part-time level. In all, 1,200 students were enrolled on the 1994–5 course making the OU the largest single provider of PGCE courses in England and Wales. It is extremely likely, with its excellent record in the production of distance-learning materials, that the support materials produced by the OU team for its students will be bought and used in other institutions. Already, in the first six months of the course, the team has produced useful material on mentoring and readers on the teaching of mathematics and English. They will also be a source of up-to-date classroom video materials. Its influence is therefore likely to spread well beyond its registered students.

Interestingly enough, this latest, and in some ways the most radical of the new routes into teaching, is advertised as being 'not available in Scotland', even though Scotland with its widely spread and small populations in the Highlands and Islands areas has been a country where the Open University has been a valued route into higher education. This is because the rigour of the training requirements for teachers, regulated by the General Teaching Council, would not make such a route an appropriate one. Indeed, the evidence of registration is that few teachers, trained outside Scotland, tend to find teaching posts there. In the period November 1990 to March 1991, for example, only seven secondary teachers from the European Community were admitted to the register as teachers in Scotland and six of those were teachers of a modern foreign language.

The OU PGCE scheme, which started in January 1994, is interesting in its own right. It has a number of distinctive features. First of all it is a course that lasts a total of eighteen months. This is because the OU's academic year is unusual in running from January to December. Thus students on the course are able to complete eighteen months of study and are still able to qualify to move into their first teaching posts in the following autumn.

The course is supported by the OU's regional structure and the students have to negotiate and obtain their own teaching placements in their home area. The schools are paid for their participation and, at the end of the course, they were given, when the scheme was first introduced, the Apple computers that the students had used during the period of training. This extra payment 'in kind' is, so far as we know, unique in the field of teacher education and is an example of another and older, almost bartering, market economy.

In a lecture he gave in 1993 Professor Bob Moon of the Open University points out that the course they are about to run:

> . . . provides an alternative routeway, but importantly not one that is in competition with existing provision. The average entry age to PGCE courses in Britain has been creeping upwards but a sample survey suggests that very few existing applicants have obtained graduate status through part-time study. It is possible, therefore, to talk about a complementary, rather than a competitive relationship between the new routeway and established practice.

Moon goes on to discuss some of the ways in which this complementary relationship might operate and concludes:

> . . . perhaps most significantly, there is an opportunity to develop models of collaboration at the implementation stage which would be of mutual benefit to a local institution and the Open University . . . The student and mentor partnership will be supported through a local tutor who in many existing courses is working part-time whilst holding a position in a local institution of HE.

This might go some way to alleviate the increasing problems of redundancy of existing HEI lecturing staff as ever more and more of their work is transferred to the schools. Another point is that the possibilities of using the well-established techniques of distance learning with which the OU is concerned are potentially very exciting in the new field of initial teacher training. Bob Moon shows himself well aware of this within the potential patterns of European collaboration:

> A number of the new IUFMs in France, for example, are looking at the potential of the technology associated with 'distance

education' in designing new courses. Universities in Poland and Hungary have explored with the Open University the potential for cooperation in the larger scale reorganizations of teacher education envisaged.

The Government Initiatives and Criticism

Whilst it would be inviting to mount a demolition attack upon the limitations of the school-based models, it seems more profitable to point to the positive values of continuing with some elements of the academic tradition such as the OU scheme provides. The case for this has been well put by John Furlong, who himself was in earlier times one of the advocates of some forms of school-based training, as shown in the report on the role of the school in initial teacher training he and other associates presented to the Department of Education and Science (Furlong *et al.*, 1988). Five years later, however, he wrote in the *Times Educational Supplement* of 29 January 1993 that:

> School-based courses give students an in-depth training in one or at the best two schools. What higher education institutions and their staff can offer is a broader perspective that comes from the involvement of [their] staff in a large number of schools, through their familiarity with current literature in the field, through their access to libraries and specialist facilities and through their active involvement in research. It is this breadth of experience that tutors bring to the courses they run and to their visits to schools. It is access to this broader perspective that helps students develop an understanding of the principles on which they work. Students cannot work by generalised principles alone but a breadth of perspective is a vital complement to the particularity of training that schools provide. Without access to the broader perspective that higher education can provide we run the risk of producing a profession that is ever more inward-looking. (Furlong, *TES*, 29 January 1993)

We thoroughly concur with this view and would only add that, with the many technological changes taking place both outside and inside the school system, to which we have already referred and which affect all aspects of education, the present is perhaps the very worst time for this 'inward-looking' stance to characterize the teaching profession. This view is strongly supported by most of the teachers' unions in their comments on the Government's proposals. For example, the Association of Teachers and Lecturers (ATL) said in *The Education of a Profession* (October, 1993) that:

The Government has taken the most serious decision to pass the
responsibility for training teachers for the next century to teachers
of this . . . If the next century finds the professionalism they in-
herit wanting, then the cause will be the value assigned to it in
these proposals. (ATL, 1993)

Similarly, the National Union of Teachers (NUT) comments in its
*Response to the Government's Proposals for the Reform of Initial Teacher Edu-
cation* (March 1992) that:

The teaching force of the 21st century will . . . be required to be
well qualified in terms of expertise, knowledge of subjects, theoretical understanding and with the personal qualities to engage,
enthuse and motivate all pupils . . . [This] will place considerable
demands upon any system and suggests that any initial training
cannot and should not be seen as a mere 'preparation for work',
divorced from the cultural and theoretical bases underpinning
practical and subject-specific skills. (NUT, 1992)

This has been recognized as far away as New Zealand. Writing in
Elliott (1993), R.G. Munro of the University of Auckland, quotes appro-
vingly the work of Barry Macdonald who:

views young teachers as having great potential as curriculum innovators, sees '. . . apprenticeship as induction into obsolete practice' and school-based training as closing '. . . yet another door to
teacher-led development'. (Munro in Elliott, 1993)

Macdonald argues for a dramatic radicalization of the training process
to enable young teachers to realize their full potential and thus contribute
to improved practices in schools. He asks:

What would such radicalization look like? In my view the answer
to this is sharply opposed to the apprenticeship context of the
trainees. We should think, rather, of the trainee as a student of
schooling, a critical and reflective observer and theorist of its contemporary conditions, practices and beliefs. . . . Initial training
should emphasize investigation of local communities, study of
children in non-school settings, case studies of schools and their
practice. We should train students in investigating and reporting curriculum issues embedded in realities of contemporary
schooling . . . In time such a trend would lead to the integration
of pre-service, in-service and school development activities into
a unified system. And within such a system the isolation of

academic theorising would break down as the roles of trainee, trainer and researcher become merged in a shared focus. (Macdonald, 1984)

This seems a much more positive vision and one that will fit the schools to become places of change rather than ones that celebrate the mores and culture of the past.

The words of the social anthropologist, Margaret Mead, in her important book, *Culture and Commitment* (1970), where she makes a useful distinction between what she called post-figurative and pre-figurative cultures, can be directly applied to two concerns which seem especially important in Macdonald's thinking:

> We must . . . teach ourselves how to alter adult behavior so that we can give up postfigurative upbringing . . . and discover pre-figurative ways of teaching and learning that will keep the future open. We must create new models for adults who can teach their children *not what to learn, but how to learn and not what they should be committed to but the value of commitment.*
>
> Postfigurative cultures, which focused on the elders — those who had learned the most and were able to do the most with what they had learned — were essentially closed systems that continually replicated the past. *We must now move towards the creation of open systems that focus on the future* — and so on children, those whose capacities are least known and whose choices must be left open. [our emphasis] (Mead, 1970)

The first is a recognition of what the student brings to the process of training — students are not simply empty vessels to be filled with the culture of schools (or, even worse, of a single school) as they may be becoming at present. It has been shown elsewhere in a case study of one PGCE course (Adams, 1991) that students can be innovators and change agents in the school where they are themselves undergoing school-practice experience. There will be the views they bring to bear upon the classroom experience which are as valid as those of the school-based mentor and which they need to discuss together; there will be the skills they can bring, in the field of information technology for example, where they will act as the mentor with the school teacher, sometimes the college tutor also, becoming the trainee. The students will also, through their work in HEIs, often possess knowledge beyond that possessed by their mentors: they are likely, for example, to know, in the field of English, more about post-modernist criticism and about linguistic theory than many established school teachers who were trained before these were increasingly the common currency of university English courses. Similarly, modern foreign-language students can be more conversant with the up-to-date idiom of the target language than their mentors and act as models in the production of teaching materials.

The essential weakness of the mentorship model is the 'client' position in which it places the student who is devalued and put, inevitably, in another's territory (the school) at a disadvantage. We prefer to this uneven distribution of power something more like what has been described by Australian practitioners as a 'triad' (Turney C. *et al.*, 1985) a mutually supportive team of student, teacher and HEI lecturer, where the power structure will shift as the opportunities and the situations shift and change. For this it is vital that all three work together in both kinds of institutions, school and HEI.

We know of cases at present where HEI-based tutors have been forbidden to see students teaching in the classroom and where serving teachers no longer come into and work alongside tutors in HEIs. The new financial arrangements and related administrative difficulties of releasing teachers or HEI staff inherent in the budgetary policies of the new initial teacher training (ITT) arrangements place further obstacles to the process. The loss on both sides is immense, even in the best of circumstances; in the worst of circumstances we have to ask what happens when the relationship between mentor and trainee breaks down. All who have been engaged in traditional models of initial teacher education will recall instances when they have had to intervene to 'protect' a student who was being unfairly or insensitively treated in a school: there is no guarantee that a gifted teacher of school pupils will be equally successful in dealing with a student in higher education.

As already indicated the vogue in the later 1970s in teacher education in England and Wales has been the idea of partnership, with schools and HEIs required to work together to forge new patterns for cooperation. There is, of course, nothing intrinsically novel about this idea. Ever since teacher education, involving HEIs, began, there have been links between the schools and the other institutions, which developed especially strongly in the Anglo-American tradition. It is difficult to see, in rational terms, how things could be otherwise. No-one has ever supposed that it is possible to prepare teachers for their work without their entering classrooms. Schools are in a very real sense the laboratory in which theories and ideas about teaching have to be tried out and the context in which teaching is put into practice. What we have seen in the late 1980s in England, however, is an interference for ideological reasons with this natural growth of collaboration, proposals for new patterns of work which impose new styles of 'partnership' upon both schools and HEIs, together with a determined attempt, often as much resisted by the schools as by the HEIs themselves, to install the schools as the senior members of the partnership.

Most of the teachers' unions and professional associations are very clear about where they stand on this and are resistant to the worst excesses of governmental proposals. The following comment by the National Union of Teachers, the largest of the teachers' unions, on their idea of partner-ship, not far removed from the situation which had existed quite success-fully throughout the 1950s and 1960s so far as teacher education was concerned, is illuminating:

> Both partners, teachers and college tutors, need to establish an integrated blend of theory and practice, where reading, research and reflection supports classroom practice . . . Though the Union believes that teachers should be involved in the training of future members of their profession, it does not support the Govern-ment's recommendation that they 'should be in the lead in the whole of the training process' . . . Colleges and schools should be involved in an equal partnership, which contains a mutual respect for differing roles. It is this quality of partnership on which good teacher education depends.

We examine later in this chapter what such partnership actually looked like at its best and the way in which schools and HEIs could quite happily divide up their separate roles in the processes of teacher education. The new element which entered into the debate in the mid-1990s has made this dynamic collaboration well-nigh impossible. In May 1994 the Govern-ment introduced the second reading of the latest Education Bill into the House of Commons. The TTA, to which we have already referred exten-sively, in Chapter 2, more than ever before transfers the processes of teacher training to the schools, who will be able to buy in expertise from HEIs and elsewhere, if they wish to do so, but will not be in any way compelled to do this. The determination of the Government to have its way was shown in that, when the House of Lords amended the Bill by a narrow majority of three to compel schools developing their own pro-grammes of teacher training to have an HEI 'partner', the Government reversed this decision on second reading and returned to its original intention.

Already, beginning in 1993, we saw the planning of experimental teacher-training programmes, for an initial cohort of 250 students, with 100 per cent of the trainees' time spent in the schools. In introducing the second reading of his Bill the Secretary of State made it clear that this scheme was to be extended in 1995 and that there was to be a wider application of it to teacher training for the primary schools as well. All this, again, before any evaluation of the first year's experiment had been completed.

The totally school-based schemes, known as School Centred Initial Teacher Training Schemes (SCITT), began in autumn 1993. In 1993–4 there was certainly one scheme operating, with eighteen students, in Bromley in Kent, where there was no link at all with an HEI, except at the examining level, when it invited three members of staff from the

Cambridge University Department of Education (acting in a personal capacity) to be external examiners. It was exactly the kind of scheme which would have been illegal if the Lords' amendment had been upheld. Though this scheme had a number of other interesting features, nevertheless, the main fact remains that it was the first fully working example of a pattern of teacher education in which the idea of partnership with HEIs had totally disappeared. We have moved a long way from what was the received wisdom until the mid-1980s.

By January 1994 there were 200 students on nine such schemes, generally based on consortia of schools. In the spring of 1994 the Secretary of State approved a further six new consortia and by 1994–5 it is intended that there will be fifteen consortia aiming to have 450 students in total.

To complete the argument of this chapter we need to examine what is likely to be lost under such schemes and what traditional elements of teacher education actually contribute to the partnership between HEIs and schools as they have emerged over the past thirty years or so.

The Best of the Old

The answer to this lies, in our view, in the roles of two key people: the 'Methods' lecturer in the HEI, and the 'supervising teacher' in the school. Whilst these are both well-established terms, it will be useful to attempt a definition of how we understand them since they have tended to be used in somewhat differing ways in different institutions.

By the 'Methods' lecturer, we mean a specialist in the teaching of a particular subject or age range, in recent years invariably someone who has had extensive and successful teaching experience in schools and who, in the new role to be assumed in the HEI, will be engaged in the development of theoretical ideas in the teaching of the subject or age range concerned, generally contributing to its development through writing and research. This role is one that has been of great significance within the Anglo-American tradition of teacher education though one that has had much less prominence in teacher-education programmes on the continental mainland of Europe. With the loss of partnership the research will be less closely linked with direct classroom experience. It should be added that, although 'Methods' lecturers have been with us for many years, it is only in relatively recent times in England and Wales that they have become fully established academic members of the staff of all HEIs. The Department of Educational Studies in the University of Oxford, for example, appointed its first 'Methods' staff with university tenure in the late 1970s; prior to that it employed school teachers on short-term contracts of three to five years who were thereafter expected to return to the classroom.

The development of the idea of the full-time HEI-based 'Methods' lecturer with full tenure and the same status as other lecturers in HEIs was one of the main features of the success of the system of teacher education in England and Wales and it lay at the very heart of the partnership between the two central institutions in the preparation of teachers for the classroom and the school. It is a position which is now being developed in some countries of mainland Europe.

The other element we have identified as the 'supervising teacher'. By this we mean an experienced teacher in the subject or age range concerned, in secondary schools often, though not necessarily, a head of department, who regularly received student teachers into the school and who acted as their supervisor during their school-practice period. During this time, which in a one-year course generally lasted for the equivalent of a school term of about ten to twelve weeks (though there were many different patterns by which this was achieved), the students would also be visited on a regular basis by their 'Methods' lecturer enabling a close working partnership to develop between the lecturers and the supervising teachers. The formal institutionally based partnership was complemented by a partnership at a personal level between two 'experts', both of whom concerned with the professional development of the student teacher. In theory, the work of the student was enhanced by, on the one hand, access to the broad experience of many schools of the 'Methods' lecturer and the in-depth experience of a few schools of the supervising teacher. In addition, 'Methods' lecturers would often work in the schools alongside the supervising teachers, engaged in trying out new classroom approaches and conducting research; similarly, the supervising teachers would often come into the HEIs, in a role often designated as 'Teacher Tutors', to supplement the work being done by the 'Methods' lecturers.

At its best this kind of partnership worked very well. It was essentially symbiotic and worked to the benefit of both partners as well as to that of the students. Many supervising teachers in due course became 'Methods' lecturers themselves and the profession of teacher education became continuously renewed in this way. The essential differences between this and the proposals being made in the 1990s are that what we have been describing were essentially partnerships of people, not institutions, they were entered into willingly rather than being forced upon the participants by administrative decree. The latter has effectively sought to introduce a 'businesslike' relationship into something that was aimed at essentially a *professional* relationship dependent upon trust and goodwill. Sometimes, of course, these relationships did not work, in which case the partnership could be dissolved by mutual agreement, often with the several partners finding new partners elsewhere.

We argue that all this benefitted both the development of expertise and new ideas about the teaching of subjects and age ranges and for the better development of the student teacher, confirmed by recent examples of Anglo-American classroom-based research. An example of our own work in this respect is discussed in Chapter 9.

The fundamental principles to be invoked in choosing a particular department for the teaching-practice placement of a student included the suitability of that school to the perceived needs of that student and the quality of supervision in the subject, or age range, that the student would receive in that department or school. In other words, all the decisions were human, not, as is now all too often the case, administrative ones. They perceived the preparing teacher as a student who had still to be educated as well as trained. Students were on the receiving end of the endeavours of a team of educators combining their differing expertise to the mutual benefit of all. A detailed account of how this worked in practice in the experience of lecturers in one UDE is given in Adams and Hadley (1982).

There were inevitably in the context just described tensions and problems: there was always the danger of an 'overloading' of the supervising teachers in the schools who generally did their work from a sense of goodwill rather than for payment. However the goodwill that existed on both sides enabled the various patterns that developed to work effectively. The publication by the Government of Circular 3/84 (DES, op.cit.), changed all this by imposing a legal framework within which teacher education would henceforward be required to operate.

The Secretary of State at the time, Sir Keith Joseph, could not interfere directly with the autonomy of universities to teach their own courses; he could, however, since Qualified Teacher Status (QTS) was granted not by the HEIs directly but through the holder of his office decree that only courses approved by CATE would enable their students to receive QTS. This very powerful weapon of control was introduced without any recourse to Parliament. As a consequence a minimum length of time for courses of ITT was laid down, well in excess of conventional university terms; criteria were established for the content of ITT courses which became subject to visits by HMI to ensure that these were complied with; and lecturers were required to return on a regular basis to the classroom to undertake 'recent and relevant experience'. Most of what was now required under the CATE regulations had already been going on as part of the cooperative relationships that had developed between HEIs and schools. The rather too ready acquiescence by the HEIs, especially the universities, in formalizing these changes undoubtedly paved the way for the subsequent introduction by the DFE of the continuing series of 'reforms' in ITT in Britain that are the subject of this part of the book.

To summarize the argument so far we would agree that issues to do with classroom management and control can only be learned in real classrooms, irrespective of the subject taught. It follows, therefore, that how to teach a particular subject in a particular classroom can only be learned in the real context of that classroom. However, prospective teachers will not work in the same classroom for the whole of their professional lives (unlike the nineteenth-century pupil teacher, and many teachers up to

World War II, who frequently did so). The job of the 'Methods' lecturers with their wider perspective is precisely to mediate between the student experience of the teaching practice classroom, or classrooms, and the wider range of schools which the student teacher will inevitably encounter. We would disagree with the view that the wider perspective will be best learned during the first years of teaching. Many newly trained teachers take up posts in schools very similar to those in which they have had their main practice experience, many are indeed appointed to posts in those very same schools. It is important that in the initial training stage their horizons are widened so that they gain some awareness of the full range of educational provision.

We should add that the term 'Methods' lecturer is used above only because this is usually the official designation within the HEI. For many years lectures, as such, have been cut to a minimum and have been replaced by 'workshops', extended teaching periods where the students learn through working alongside each other and their lecturers engaged in a variety of tasks such as lesson planning and the preparation of teaching materials. In course planning thought has to be given to what can be best learned in the school and what is more appropriate to the HEI.

The problem with the new largely, or wholly, school-based courses is that much of the best of what has been described above is lost. The range of experience for the trainee is likely to be less; they are exposed to fewer people; they lack the support of a peer group in the same subject area on whom to try out ideas. Our experience so far of such courses, especially the entirely school-based ones, is that they are excessively concerned with classroom management in one or two schools and that little attention is given to thinking through such issues as what we are teaching, why we are teaching it, or how it might be taught in a different classroom or school. In a nutshell, the focus is necessarily too narrow and the teacher turns out to be trained but not educated. The new arrangements may exclude a direct experience of certain types of school, such as those in multicultural cities, which may not feel able to join the new ITT schemes, thus depriving students of a vital experience hitherto generally built into HEI-organized schemes. The reason for our insistence above on the role of the prospective teacher as 'student' is linked with what necessarily follows from the patterns of teacher education that have been described, principles that were established as early as the James Report with which we dealt in Chapter 2.

In contrast to recent practice in mainland European countries the present proposals in England and Wales are tending to compress all this into the initial training stage alone. At the same time as policies are moving in this direction, the probationary year has been abolished and LMS has meant a significant decrease in any in-service work which is seen in a wider context than that of the individual school.

A final comment on these issues draws upon the experience of someone who has been both a supervising teacher (though she here uses the word 'mentor') and a 'Methods' lecturer (which she calls a 'curriculum tutor') — as indeed have both the authors of the present book:

> Having shifted from being a mentor to a curriculum tutor I began to appreciate how very different the roles are. Mentors contribute specific classroom expertise, school support, knowledge of their pupils, curriculum knowledge. Curriculum tutors contribute general, de-contextualised knowledge and an oft-needed 'neutrality' . . . . Anecdotes about my own experience in the classroom could only go so far. A broader and much more disciplined approach was necessary. Distilling complicated research findings, choosing the most relevant reading, provoking, challenging, affirming, are all parts of the tutor's demanding job. (Hake, 1993)

All those of us who have made this transition will recognize what is referred to here. It should remind us also that student teachers are undergoing a similar transition. They are moving in a short time, often less than a calendar year, from being a receiver to being a provider of the educational system. For them to achieve this transition successfully it is essential that they are supported by a complementary team of teacher educators and teacher trainers. Neither one nor the other alone will be sufficient to the purpose.

A significant further element that is important in the kind of vision that Macdonald sketched in the extract quoted earlier is that students trained in the way he suggests are more likely to extend similar respect to the school pupils whom they are teaching. They need to recognize that these pupils are individuals who bring their own skills, interests, and areas of knowledge to the classroom. It is a truism, which also happens to be true, that in a classroom where there are thirty pupils there are also thirty experts on something or other. It may be that the knowledge, experience and skills that the school pupil brings into the situation is not always valued by the school. This is one of the elements which explains the alienation from the institution of school that many young people feel. Significantly Macdonald points to the importance of the 'study of children in non-school setting'. It is precisely the fact that so much is wrong with the institution of schooling that makes wholly school-based training the wrong way to prepare the next generation of teachers.

It may be noted that, after the introduction of the extended PGCE course to a period of thirty-six weeks, the opportunity was taken in the Cambridge course to introduce an element known as 'Extended Professional Experience'. This enabled students in the last weeks of their course to engage in aspects of education which could be outside the classroom altogether. This might involve, for example, teaching in a prison, taking part in field courses, working at the Museum of the Moving Image in

London, or undertaking a variety of teaching experiences abroad. The students and lecturers concerned felt that this was an invaluable opportunity to recognize that much education went on outside the formal institution of schooling. They also learned different aspects of a teacher–pupil relationship. Unhappily, this kind of enterprise is no longer possible given the Government's insistence upon a twenty-four-week *school-based* element to the course.

Another Debate

The advocates of the school-based model, notably Hargreaves in Tulasiewicz *et al.* (1992), and in the Hockerill Lecture (Hargreaves, 1990), discussed at length in Elliott (1993), is that they assume that all is well with the institution of schooling, that more of the same will do. In so doing, they effectively disenfranchise and devalue both HEI and school pupils. Writing in Elliott (op.cit.), who is not such an advocate, Hargreaves makes this crystal-clear:

> Teachers . . . have two dominant concerns, which I shall treat as sectors that are part of every teacher's professional knowledge and professional development. The first sector concerns their performance as a teacher, and the second that of the performance of pupils. (Hargreaves in Elliott, 1993)

He goes on to identify five segments in each of these sectors which parallel each other in terms of the teacher- and pupil-performance sectors. The first of these speaks of, on the one hand:

> class management: the teacher's authority, and ability to control and organise the classroom

and, on the other:

> Pupil behaviour and conformity: acceptance of teacher authority and manageability

Obviously no-one would argue for an uncontrolled classroom as being a good in itself but the language here of 'conformity' and 'acceptance of authority' goes well beyond this. This is the language of manipulation: the kind of approach which suppresses children and produces the compliant citizenry which is the real aim of the New Right, however much Hargreaves in his rhetoric seeks to distance himself from it.

In the same volume Hargreaves disputes Elliott's interpretation of his ideas with some asperity. The debate in print between Elliott and

Hargreaves is a curious reprise of that between Hirst and Simon to which we referred in Chapter 2. But whereas the earlier was conducted with mutual respect and a tone of academic moderation, the present debate is much more marked by ill-temper and impatience.

In all that he has written on these matters, however, Hargreaves seems deterministically to take for granted that the whole scale changes that have taken place in the structure of education which we have mentioned at the start of this chapter (the National Curriculum, Local Management of Schools (LMS), the decline of the Local Education Authorities (LEA)) are both necessary and irreversible. For all the boldness and coherence his, like that of the New Right, is essentially a position that leads to conservatism and sterility in education; it has no vision for a future for education that will be able to meet the momentous opportunities of the New Europe and the New Century. For that Macdonald, writing more than fifteen years earlier, may well prove the truer prophet.

Part 2

Comparative Perspectives

Chapter 5

Comparative Methods

Introduction

Conventional accounts of teacher education dealing with more than one country generally consist of short thumbnail sketches of factual information, such as the available institutions, the length of courses, their location, the dates and reasons for the introduction of relevant legislation, and a brief general description of actual practice.

Accessible public information does not provide the full facts necessary to make meaningful comparisons or to indicate borrowings from foreign practice. The only possible discussion turns out to be one about language rather than substance.

A thematic analysis is needed to attempt a valid comparative study showing the complete pattern of practice adopted and the impact of any changes that might be introduced. Such an analysis will examine in detail the discrete components which make up the teacher-preparation courses being looked at and their separate development before comparing their relation and relevance to each other. If lessons are to be drawn, these developments must be seen embedded in their respective socio-cultural contexts and checks made for similarities in the contexts of the other sets compared.

In what follows these contexts will be sketched in as appropriate. A more complete background for all the interconnected structures and practices referred to is not possible within the compass of this book, the purpose of which is to use comparison to achieve a better understanding of British practice rather than propose educational borrowing.

Terminology and Context

An important first requirement for a valid examination is the ability to use the different terminology. For example the full meaning of such terms as 'secondary education' or 'education theory' is often not understood even by those who participate in the work of the relevant institutions and who share in educational decision-making. Admittedly, there may be fewer problems when translating such terms as 'comprehensive schooling', '*Realschule*', or the French '*collège*'. 'Primary', 'elementary' or 'middle-school education' may be more complicated considering the different starting points and syllabuses taught; indeed, how does one render 'education' into German when there are at least three terms: *Erziehung, Bildung,* and *Unterricht* to choose from, and the context of each will immediately reveal the existence of other English terms? American terminology can supply many other words for further consideration, such as 'school' in the sense of 'college' for example.

Teacher educators outside the two countries concerned are unlikely to be familiar with the precise and different contents of a French and a Dutch *agrégation* even though they may know its timing, coming, as it does, at the end of a teacher's training course. The same goes for the exact content of the Spanish postgraduate certificate of teacher training, the *Certificado de Aptitud Pedagogica* and its conditions for admission; or indeed the names and functions of different teacher categories in the member states of the European union. This difficulty is only beginning to be resolved by specialist lexicons such as that being produced by Jean Marie de Ricolfis for the Institut National de Recherche Pédagogique (INRP) or similar publications on topics of educational practice commissioned by the Council of Europe in Strasbourg, one or two of which are referred to by us elsewhere in this volume.

The second comparative tool is an effective description of educational structures and their practical functions compared in context, which enables them to be seen, as it were, in action, rather than statically. The following brief descriptions of two features common in teacher-preparation courses are designed to enable an appreciation of the issues involved in each revealing their inherent dynamic and demonstrating the use of the comparative instrument in the practical examples studied.

1   Of the two types of teacher preparation courses traditionally referred to as consecutive and concurrent, the consecutive model, well known in the English version of the Postgraduate Certificate of Education, may be said to be on the increase. After the recently introduced reforms in France which extend initial, pre-service professional training to all prospective school teachers holding a *licence* from a University, the consecutive model is the one adopted in the courses on offer in the *Instituts Universitaires de Formation des Maîtres* (IUFMs) introduced in 1991. Unlike the content of the courses, the professional merits of consecutive preparation do not appear to have been widely discussed before adoption. To be sure, in the early 1980s, the UK Government (DES, 1982) viewed the consecutive model as less wasteful than the concurrent one of resources invested in students, if, at the end of their professional course of study, a certain number decided not to take up teaching as a career. In France, compared with the UK, the pre-selection of certain quotas for teaching posts before proceeding with training

makes such an outcome less likely. Drawbacks of the consecutive models, such as the more limited time available for professional work since they are as a rule shorter than concurrent ones, their timing and rather in-service flavour, or indeed the advantage of keeping students' options open for longer before they decide on a teaching career, did not figure much in the planning of these courses, scheduled to admit graduates only. The recent extension of the term of initial training in Germany to two years has as much to do with the availability of financial resources and the need for teachers as it has with the extra time released for the preparation of qualified professionals in a situation where not all those trained will proceed to take up a teaching job.

2   The widely used term 'professional theory' distinguishes between educational theory such as history of education taught as part of the personal, liberal education which can be received in HEIs, and theory more directly relevant to classroom teaching, such as sub-ject teaching methods, which in Britain has been taught both in HEIs prior to teaching experience or, in school, during actual teaching practice. The use of the term 'theory' to describe the latter is, however, less common.

Even so, the demarcation lines are not very clear except where the consecutive practical preparation phase is completely separate from that of academic study. The Anglo-American tradition of close links between HEIs and practice schools, including the exchange of personnel, has blurred this distinction, resulting in some overlap, but, as against that, is responsible for producing a considerable volume of educational literature on the distinctive qualities of theory and practice, available and required, and the preparation of the teaching personnel involved. The generally neat separation of theory and professional preparation in Germany has worked against this practice, resulting in a smaller volume of available and relevant major professional research and literature of this nature, much of which often amounts to little more than helpful hints for classroom techniques or is much influenced by American and British models.

In England, theory began to attract criticism when it was taught by academically qualified staff with little or no profes-sional classroom-teaching experience. There is some agreement, but no unanimity that there can be no successful subject teaching if teachers are ignorant of the social composition of their classes and the context of their schools, which require some knowledge of the sociology and psychology of education. The question who should teach this theory, if it is to be taught, hinges on the differ-ent status of the lecturers involved and the conditions for their appointment to a university or school-training post. In England these are different from those in Scotland, for example, where all teaching and teacher-training appointments have to be registered according to criteria laid down by the General Teaching Council.

3   The third tool is the need for caution before advocating educational borrowing. The illustration is of cases of actual borrowing from one context into a new one, where the transplants do not appear to have taken root.

Comparisons of educational structures actually made by official agencies often finish by listing a number of similarities and models. For example: both Britain and France have a comprehensive school system. However, even a cursory glance reveals the different position at the senior-school level, which has an impact on the years of schooling immediately preceding the final years. These differences may prove to be far from superficial, as in the example of the provision of statutory alternative and supplementary tuition in basic subjects in France, which does not exist in England.

The recent studies of education in Europe in the 1980s conducted by HMI may have provided an impetus for the articled-teacher scheme being introduced in England and Wales but they did not anticipate the high cost of the reform nor the problems associated with employing, under contract, trainee teachers from the start of their training programmes. What is common practice in Germany may not take when tried out in England, given the difference in terms of employment, pay, traditional locations and length of courses and the status of both the teaching personnel employed and the trainees.

Educational Borrowing and Innovation

The advocacy of new alternative teacher-training routes, such as the licensed training scheme offering a faster route to professional preparation through practical classroom training, which was introduced and subsequently abandoned in several areas of the United States (such as Ohio and Michigan), partly because of professional pressure, could only be tried out in England because regulations governing entry to the profession could be changed wholesale by government regulation. The professional teacher-training scheme in New Jersey has been strongly supported by several British educationalists on the right of the political spectrum (Lawlor, op.cit.), with little account taken of one of the principal reasons for its introduction there: the acute general teacher shortage in that part of America at the time.

The proposals described above are literally copies of measures introduced abroad, as an immediate response to problems, with little detailed assessment of their suitability under British conditions. In different circumstances such ignorance can lead to the partial breakdown of promising collaborative schemes, for example the European-union student and student-teacher exchanges referred to in Part 3.

Knowledge of educational structures and processes can be improved through investigating their origins which reveals that the similarity of important features of practices and policies, may be only superficial, apparent rather than real. This also applies to institutional practices, such as the organization of teacher education. Though their origin may owe much to the thoughts of internationally respected educational thinkers, their impact is largely determined by the actual situation found in their nation state.

The location of teacher education, whether received in a secondary (normal) school, as is still the case in the training of preschool teachers in the Netherlands, in a specialist teacher-education college (likely in the case of most elementary-school teachers), or in a university (often for teachers who will be working with the most senior classes) can tell us much about the emphasis given to the different parts of teacher preparation — the academic and the professional; the theoretical and the practical — often invoked in comparisons of teachers' prestige and influence. Where these differences persist they take little account of the actual demand of trained personnel, for example in the absence of a large selective school sector.

The training situation in England, with its large and prestigious private-school sector, seems to take less account of differentiated training than the Netherlands do, where their numerous private schools are far less influential in public life. Indeed, much teacher-preparation provision seems to be geared for teachers who will be taking up posts in the upper forms of elite schools, for example the *lektors* in Norway. The Dutch model of a non-university, but integrated (that is catering for both academic and professional training) institution of higher education, the *pedagogische akademie*, introduced in 1970, is interesting. It allows university graduates (that is the prospective teachers for the academic VWO schools which prepare pupils aged 12 to 18 for universities) to receive their consecutive professional and practical half-year training in the same *akademie* as all other teachers, whose own training, though longer, is concurrent with their academic work, which the future VWO teachers absolve in the university.

It is important to appreciate the difference between the intrinsically important and the outwardly attractive, as in the question whether teacher preparation is predominantly the pursuit of academic, or of professional, expertise and excellence.

Chapter 6

Teachers' Professional Status and Prestige

Training and Status

Separating the training of teachers according to their future pupils' ages and ability may be justified by enabling greater concentration upon topics of essential concern to a particular section of the profession. If the locations used for this are different, this policy may affect the status of both the trainees and the trainers involved, depending on the prestige enjoyed by the institution in which the training takes place. The notion of institutional prestige may be perceived as a peculiarly English feature, but it can also be found in the prestige enjoyed by such institutions as the *grandes écoles* in France or reflected in the vastly differing facilities available in the *Instituts Universitaires de Formation des Maîtres* (IUFMs) some of which had to be found inferior accomodation at short notice by their *académies*.

Equality of prestige and status in teacher preparation, as well as the need for an improved professional preparation, were the reasons for establishing the IUFMs in the first place. The subsequent reduction, under the conservative Balladur administration, of the amount of psycho-pedagogical theory taught in the IUFMs in favour of more subject discipline knowledge taught in both the IUFMs and the universities in teacher-preparation courses meant for future secondary-school teachers, lessened the impact of the original legislation intended to give the same professional preparation to all teachers.

The shift in involvement by the IUFMs away from the professional and practical side, welcomed by the unions also had implications for the prestige of the profession as a whole. Recent English legislation, setting up the Teacher Training Agency and locating most of teachers' professional preparation in schools rather than in universities, has certainly been criticized by many who saw it solely in terms of lowering professional academic prestige and overlooking the power shift in teacher preparation which accompanied it.

Teachers as Civil Servants

Civil-servant status is generally assumed to confer security of tenure and to ensure a say in the negotiation of conditions of service, such as the hours worked, salaries paid and entitlement to benefits not available to employees whose conditions of employment have to be negotiated separately every time a new fixed-term post is accepted. In the western democracies civil servants are protected by the full backing of their professional and vocational organizations in case of dispute. Moreover, by virtue of their status they become involved, as of right, in the various consultation processes, not only in discussions of their conditions of service, but subject to their levels of seniority, office and competence, in discussions of the merits of policies proposed for legislation. The 50–50 principle of representation in consultations is important, even if in the course of discussions, ways may be found to effectively limit the contributions made by those *professionals who are civil servants* compared with those made by *professional civil servants*, the latter in Germany jokingly called *Kal Faktoren*.

The remuneration of trainee teachers as civil servants may have immediate financial benefits, although, by being placed in a particular post after qualifying, the new diploma holders' freedom of choice of professional job, affecting their future careers, is reduced. This is well-known in the case of *lycée* teachers in France who are often assigned their first teaching posts far away from their place of residence. As against that, the competitive entry examinations (the *concours*) in France ensure that there are teaching posts for all newly qualified teachers after their studies, a security German teachers enjoy only for a limited initial period after completing their studies. Compared with other professionals, teachers' standing as a rule is too low to enable them, as freelance experts, to demand attractive contracts negotiated by themselves as self-employed workers. In England teachers are increasingly being appointed to limited tenure positions.

Working for the State, in Poland and Germany for example, teachers are required to swear an oath of loyalty which removes their right to belong to organizations not approved by the State and to strike. These terms may be a burden, particularly as regards restriction on membership of certain political parties and other associations. On the other hand the need for teachers ensures that they are often allowed to carry on by their employers largely unchecked. It may be a matter of interest that in Poland in 1980 under the communist regime, teachers, as a small majority, were opposed to joining the ranks of the freedom-seeking trade union *Solidarność*, which had recruited 100 per cent among miners, farm workers and others.

Professional Freedom and Accountability

A comparative approach can explore the alleged constraints suffered by teachers, who, it is claimed, as civil servants, have to teach to a prescribed school curriculum determined by government officials in the *Länder* of the Federal Republic or the French *académies*. Such views are expressed by representatives of interest groups extolling the position of the independent professional. In modern France and Germany the prestige and legislated independence of the civil service have not been adversely affected despite the fact that in both countries the school curriculum has tended to be more closely prescribed over a longer period of time than in England. This is because, like parents and pupils, teachers have clearly defined rights of consultation before teaching materials are adopted. They also have a say in senior staff appointments made in the school, for example, headteachers, by the civil servants responsible. The civil servants themselves usually are qualified professionals in the relevant specialisms. A similar principle operates in the strictly delimited hierarchy of responsibility held by education inspectors in France who are in charge of teacher preparation and assessment at the different levels of *académie*, district and locality.

The principle of professional accountability has frequently enabled parents to take teachers to court for a variety of perceived derelictions of duty, such as the failure to get their child through an examination. Though more common in Germany and France than it is in England, this practice could be implemented irrespective of whether teachers are civil servants or not.

Responsibility for the curriculum is apportioned amongst several parties which normally can control each other's proposals; excesses in this respect are possible and make interesting reading, particularly the observations on the English curriculum by Denis Lawton in his *The Tightening Grip* (1984). John Tomlinson in his *Control of Education* (1993) has commented on the introduction of educational measures in England arguing that the changes introduced reflect the influence of the various groups involved in the changes proposed. This in turn depends on the shifts in the balance of power held by politicians, civil servants, teachers, professional associations and examining boards. Allowances have to be made for the fact that some of the partners involved may represent more than one interest group.

It is accepted that there has to be a degree of cooperation between their employers as controllers and teachers as implementers of innovation, notwithstanding all the other agencies and interests involved. Even so it is the government which is in a position to use its full powers to approve a school curriculum which reflects its educational priorities and ideologies by its overall control over the aims and objectives of education. Extreme examples, where teachers could not make their protests heard, such as the physical fitness and 'training of the will' programmes in Nazi Germany, or the school construction policies in Pinochet's Chile, which deprived thousands of peasants of their basic education, are fortunately rare.

In every case teachers' autonomy, whether civil servant or not, is limited by their having to teach a prescribed curriculum in a manner commensurate with broad outline norms of teaching styles and methods. What they can do, however, is to retain their own individuality of approach. In other words one can recognize a classroom the world over.

Consultation in Decision-making and Change

Most teachers and teacher trainers in mainland Europe can comment on the training syllabuses they use directly or more likely through their representatives or senior colleagues, who serve on the appropriate committees which draw up the curriculum and choose the teaching materials. Parent and pupil representatives are also entitled to a say, with the decisions made by the appropriate officials known to be responsible for them. In Germany the local parliaments, the *Landtage*, have to create committees to which the professional, union and civic interests appoint their representatives to discuss policy. In Britain, while there is much opportunity for comments to be made, there is little chance of notice being taken as seen in recent consultations over the National Curriculum and in the Universities' Council for the Education of Teachers and Committee of Vice-Chancellors and Principals' comments about teacher-training reform.

The teaching profession is more than most subject to the control and powers of intervention exercised by others. Besides governments (with full powers of legislation) there are, for example, the churches, the funding agencies and the professional associations with advisory or moral powers. The professional freedom of those practising education can, therefore, be restricted by more laws and regulations than that of other professionals (Williams, 1994). The number of pressure groups and interests proclaiming their views, some of whom, like parents, have recently gained entry onto educational advisory boards and the governing bodies of schools, where they can voice their views, has been growing faster in the Anglo-Saxon countries than in mainland Europe, where, however, their rights have been recognized earlier, as in the French *comités de l'école* and the German *Elternbeiräte*.

Detailed regulations for participation in policy decisions, the receipt of suggestions and comments, and the implementation of policies vary from country to country. Participation in advisory or consultative roles has to be distinguished from legislative powers. In France the *syndicats* were consulted in the negotiations for both the establishment and the modification of the IUFMs but the final decisions made through reflecting some of their views were not theirs. In the recent curriculum and teacher-education reform proposals in England teacher associations and unions could, and did, express opinions, as seen in their responses to the National Curriculum Council (NCC), the School Examinations and Assessment Council (SEAC), now the School Curriculum and Assessment Authority

(SCAA), and, pertinently, their comments on the reform of Initial Teacher Training, some of which we quote in Chapter 4. If at all their contribution to the debate, was only indirectly taken into account in the final decisions made, so that they became just another voice which could for the most part be ignored. In such cases regulations can clarify the position: in Germany university teachers have no statutory voice in matters of teacher education but school teachers do. Exact practice varies in the sixteen *Länder*.

Educational change has the power to activate all the agents likely to participate, whether or not they are officially involved in the decision-making. More so in England than in mainland Europe, the powers of the consumers have been widely recognized. At the same time, the professional sector has been effectively silenced. Parents can be deemed to participate when exercising their rights to withdraw their children from certain lessons; school governors do it by using their powers to regulate sex education in primary schools. Participation of business interests in the process of determining the contents of teacher preparation is being mooted in England (DES, 1989), as well as in the United States. A general comment on the change and distribution of decision-making powers in the state is made by Roche (1993).

The net effect is more open discussion and debate, exemplified in Britain in the course of 1994 by the comments on moral, sex and religious education allowed in schools, as in the guidance on sex advice to school pupils given to teachers by the then Secretary for Education in May 1994, which had to be quickly withdrawn. This was also seen in the controversy over religious education and the reaction of many of the Christian Churches to the predominantly Christian approach advocated by the Government. In Europe the civil-service tradition tends to put more of the preliminary debate out of public reach, so that the final decisions made may look less as if they had been government imposed than they do in Britain.

Despite the lively and open debate as seen in the above examples from England and Wales the greater control assumed by government over ever more aspects of education is a fact, since, unlike in the United States, non-government groups in Britain exercise little decision-making power. However, government policies and decisions are often a response to lobby pressure. In the example about contraceptive advice to be given to school pupils the complete picture must seek to reconcile the influence of the Established Church with that of other religious as well as secular moral influences pervading the English state-maintained school system and the notice taken of it by government. In France, where, as in the United States, state-maintained schools are secular, this does not prevent clashes over girls' Muslim dress worn in school in which the minister has to intervene (Tulasiewicz and To, 1993). The right of individual teachers to make decisions in such matters has recently been taken away from them. The status of religious instruction as part of the school curriculum in Poland is controversial, the Government being able to impose their solutions against a population which paradoxically is itself largely religiously committed.

The freedom of individual professionals working in education can be illustrated by experience in the former Soviet Union where teachers could close the classroom door, which had no windows through which an inspector could look uninvited, firmly behind them during lessons and produce their own detailed commentary on the school syllabus, so long as they kept to the main outlines, which were always published. The example of national testing in England reveals the outcome of teachers' work with their pupils, and its scripts are marked according to set criteria which have to be observed, the only difference being that in the UK the political bias is less in evidence.

Not surprisingly, in all societies, in times when the airing of opinion on education matters was much less common, overt control on the part of government was less resented, which in England was not excessive. Indeed, the work of public examining boards was felt to affect more people. The variety of opinions made possible especially as a result of legislation giving greater powers to the wider expression of views on the curriculum and other school matters (Education No. 2 Act, 1986; Education Reform Act, 1988; and subsequent legislation) may have made the position of British teachers more difficult. Their continental colleagues are perhaps somewhat less used to making public comments, but they are aware of the powers they do have. Not being civil servants, British teachers appear to be freer to express their views than their continental colleagues who are bound by a strictly laid-down official code of conduct.

In present circumstances, when, for a complexity of moral, religious, civic and political reasons, contrasting opinions on such topics as AIDS and homosexuality have been articulated by variously committed numerous and influential pressure groups, it is disturbing that teacher preparation, in the United Kingdom and elsewhere, has not addressed the issue of teaching controversial subjects by teachers more adequately, though this is included in the criteria listed by the Council for the Accreditation of Teacher Education (CATE). The German and French equivalents have no specific slots for this teaching except within the legal framework of school regulations. The problem of distinguishing between unrestrained freedom and control, with the requirement to present balanced views imposing limits on the professionals' freedom and autonomy, is more pertinent than ever.

Education for Professionalism in Teaching

With compulsory education a vital concern of the nation state, teachers are unlikely to be able directly to validate the content and structures of their professional preparation courses. Even so, there are differences in the freedom with which professionals can determine some aspects of their preparation. The decline of the professional voice has recently been particularly marked in Britain with the assumption of greater powers by ministers, especially by recruiting personnel to the quangos nominated by government ministers to work to a brief of their choosing. A civil-service bureaucracy while working for its government has traditionally had more respect accorded to its professional opinion. Indeed, in a bureaucratic system, the precise rights and duties of the various contracting parties are spelled out in detail leaving less room for surprise decisions made by the ministers, as in the case of recent French reforms in teacher preparation where every stage was open to public scrutiny. The fact that in England teachers are appointed by the individual governing bodies of the schools in which they teach, limits the power of the local education authority as a middle safety tier in the case of dispute to protect the teacher.

The precise role of OFSTED inspectors, a privatized body charged with monitoring a public-education system, an innovation not found in the other countries referred to in this book, has not been investigated to date. The workings of Her Majesty's Inspectorate of course have been written about (Lawton and Gordon, 1987). In mainland Europe inspections are the duty of the next up tier of civil servant nominated to make them.

A teaching profession, educated and trained entirely in HEIs, to which admission is by possession of at least a secondary school-leaving certificate, has been in existence in England, where it began to emerge with the introduction of professional training of secondary teachers in universities, for longer than in much of the rest of Europe (McNair, 1944). It could be assumed that this profession would expect to take part in debates concerning both the school curriculum and its own structure. If this did not happen, then the reason may be either because many teachers were not sufficiently equipped with the political skills to wish to participate, or because they were prevented by the absence of relevant mechanisms from the opportunity to do so. This was demonstrated by the findings of research conducted in 1990 by Tulasiewicz. In either case, it is necessary that teacher education should include, besides subject knowledge and professional preparation and induction, an element which enables teachers not just to give instruction but to be fully aware of all the circumstances of their being engaged in doing so.

Suggestions, currently heard in England, for short fixed-term contracts for teachers and a rapid turnover of teachers, with the profession diluted with the influx of personnel unqualified in professional terms (Hargreaves, 1994) are unwelcome because they further reduce teachers' professional independence. It is claimed that they give a false sense of diversity and choice, however they can only widen the gap between different sectors of professionals and thus depress standards leading to a weakening of the professional teacher's voice, a point made by Adams in a letter quoted in the introduction. Ironically this type of open criticism by a professional is less frequent outside Britain and unlikely to be given the same amount of public attention there, but is almost more likely to result in policy change if the decision to take it on board has been taken. The reasons are the different existing professional safeguards of a tenured profession which controls more of its own destiny. Teachers and teacher trainers in Britain are being confronted by the proliferating powerful supervising authorities.

The receipt of both their academic and professional education by teachers in HEIs has been at the centre of a debate on the status of major and minor professions and the place of the teaching profession among them. This debate has been especially fierce in countries like the United States (Schön, 1983), where the Anglo-American tradition of the university's responsibility for both 'theory and practice' has more or less confirmed the major status of the profession (Cremin, 1988). In France and Poland higher-education qualifications for all have been too recent to contribute significantly to remove the distinction in status of teachers in different types of school. In Germany, the civil servant ranks available to different categories of teachers differ, even though the separation between a liberal university education and a professional preparation period outside it applies to all professions and does not discriminate against teachers (Tournier, 1993).

Locating all of teachers' professional preparation primarily in schools is likely to limit the choice of English trainees in two ways: they would be forced to follow a rather narrow range of experiences in a few schools, a comment made by several English teachers' unions. They would inevitably also have failed to acquire the same degree of professional and personal maturity and assurance to enable them to take up a stand in a debate about professional standards and their own readiness to discuss the topic.

It is irksome to see the professional status of teachers in England and Wales, though not in Scotland, barely twenty-five years after the introduction of an all-graduate teaching profession, in the process of being eroded by the curtailment of opportunities for consultation, the reduction of the role of theory, and the diminution of the involvement of higher education in teacher preparation.

International educational initiatives after the Treaty on Union, such as the introduction of a European dimension in education or the SOCRATES Programme are discussed in detail in Part 3. They will affect teacher preparation in all member states. Freed from the constraints of aims seen exclusively in terms of the priorities of a single member state, it is to be hoped that the opportunity might be found for teachers and teacher educators to get together to use their internationally acknowledged and expanded professional responsibility to engage in debate before the introduction of reforms likely to affect them, raising their professional awareness and autonomy in the process. Indeed, the complex infrastructure of teachers' status merits a detailed international study in time for the review of the Treaty on Union with its educational clauses and the 'Social Chapter' in 1996.

The academic preparation now received by most teachers in the European union, may be precisely the arrival point for a profession in which teacher status has changed from that of a missionary-like concern with the younger sections of the population, a vocation, to one where the professionals are acknowledged as capable of taking their place alongside members of the other major professions, having their opinions listened to and given the necessary funding when a case for their implementation has been made out. The reasons why this potential esteem has not been fully realized everywhere may be found in the absence of an affirmation of the status of the professional preparation of teachers seen as equally strong as that of their academic and personal education.

English practice, while according the subject discipline a role in the academic curriculum similar to that found elsewhere in Europe and North America, has been responsible for allocating the professional dimension in teaching less prominence overall. This is due to the shorter length of the required combined period of academic and professional preparation courses in England and Wales compared with continental Europe (four years as against a minimum of six years excluding the probationary period).

In England and Wales this status has been further weakened by the system of exemptions from the training process, for example future graduate mathematics and science teachers do not have to be trained, though most choose to do so and are encouraged by existing bursary schemes. There is further the lack of a clear demarcation between teachers of different subjects and age groups, which allows the employment of licensed teachers who are still being trained, which is absent elsewhere, including in Scotland. The teaching of professional ethics in teacher-training courses is left entirely to the recruiting staff of teachers' unions. Politics of education is not a part of the professional preparation of teachers in England and Wales. It is taught in Canadian universities responsible for teacher training as well as in Germany and Poland.

The civil-servant status of teachers in countries of mainland Europe plus the registering powers of a teaching council have prevented the large-scale influx of variously prepared teachers on various contracts into schools. In England and Wales it is not a case of not finding a job, but finding one for which you have been trained.

A European Community Directive 89/48/EC provided for the mutual recognition by all Member States of qualifications throughout the European union by 1 January 1991. In England this was agreed by the Department of Education and Science in 1989.

Chapter 7

Educational Change and
Teacher Preparation

Characteristics of Teacher Education and Training

In the West teacher training has been characterized by several common features most of which, until not long ago, could be found in much of Europe and North America. These were:

1 a distinction between elementary and secondary training; indeed training for preschool education might constitute a third route;
2 the existence of both concurrent and consecutive models;
3 a division, sometimes to be found, according to gender, separating training facilities for men and women;
4 an involvement of the Church in teacher training, given that in many countries church-maintained schools are part of the national system with provision for the teaching of religion;
5 the relative neglect, until recently, of a practical-professional element in the preparation received by future secondary teachers;
6 the existence of an element of nation-state patriotism particularly in much of elementary teacher training and reflected in the training curriculum;
7 a competitive element in the selection of candidates who, once they qualify, achieve the status of civil servant or equivalent.

It is symptomatic of the current reforms that many of these distinctive features are disappearing. This is especially so in case of features 3 and 5, confirming the arrival of a major profession. The fourth and the sixth are being appropriated by the more fundamental regimes, especially so in the newly consolidated nation states in the Middle East and Africa which underlines the close link between education and the secular and religious establishments. A new alliance is emerging between some of the more militant religions and influential public opinion in parts of the world, such as the United States. This process will continue to grow in strength, given the financial support it receives from interest groups. There is similar support also in the countries emerging after the collapse of the former Soviet Union. The gradual disappearance of the distinctive different character of primary and secondary teachers' preparation confirms the higher professional status of teaching (Convey, 1994). Professional preparation for teaching must be seen in these contexts to enable an assessment to be made of teachers' autonomy and the professional quality of their training.

Standards and Quality

The more directly professional, as opposed to socio-political challenges, which currently confront teachers, teacher educators and educational administrators alike, and which have their roots in the new socio-political and economic constellations in Europe and not only there, arise from the changed professional expectations which may be summed up by the term *standards*, both intellectual and behavioural which they do not set themselves. Standards are affected by the availability of financial and human resources, the strength of competition, the existence of cooperation or protective measures, and the degree of quality control; all of which stem from, and lead back to, educational priorities which emerge as a result of political and ideological decisions.

In the United Kingdom, more than in other European-union member states, the current preoccupation with a market approach to education tends to invoke both standards and quality, although quality education and vocational preparation are both also the expected outcome of the introduction of the European dimension into education, resulting in streamlining of activities and economies made to paraphrase the Brussels Green Paper of 1993 on the *European Dimension of Education*. The assiduous implantation of market policies in education, is exemplified by the quantity and variety of radical curriculum and structural innovations, that have taken place since James Callaghan's Ruskin College speech in 1976 and the 'Great Debate' which he started (Tulasiewicz and Adams, 1989). The importance attached to high-quality education in Britain is more likely to be echoed in America than in mainland Europe. Apart from the party political market priorities, the reason for the similarity of this approach to educational expectations are the strong traditional links between the two major English-speaking societies and the exchange of educational experiences, of which the copying of models, such as the unlamented voucher scheme and the 'alternative routes' to teacher preparation referred to in Part 1, involving greater use made of schools for teacher training, are examples.

For historical, socio-political, and economic reasons educational change has at different times identified different educational priorities. In much of Europe this has currently led to extending the period of compulsory schooling, abolishing many of the selective schools, and introducing new subjects into the curriculum whilst at the same time financing the restructuring of its scope so as to give individual teachers more freedom to run their own lessons. In teacher education the last fifteen years or so have witnessed the increased role of higher education accompanied by the introduction of new institutions and the growth of in-service provision (Brock and Tulasiewicz, 1994). These new European directions, especially in teacher education, do not apply to England and Wales, where, as we have seen, there has been a *reduction* in higher-education participation and more government intervention accompanied by financial cut-backs.

Indeed, outlay in terms of human and financial resources devoted to the implementation of educational reform in England and Wales has not been directed to similar purposes in the other countries referred to in this book. Neither has the mood announcing the need for the changes been as adversarial. The example of the smooth change in the reduction of the psycho-pedagogic elements in the preparation of secondary teachers in the IUFMs can once again be cited in support, notwithstanding the fact that it has meant a partial return to the practice of a differentiated preparation for primary and secondary teachers in France.

What, in view of the large scale abandonment of the findings of sustained and extended professional debate in favour of often unqualified responses to government circulars, can be described as a bulldozer approach of government imposed educational change in Britain, contrasts with a detailed assessment and professional discussion of the educational elements to be changed prior to their introduction as reforms in France.

In the IUFM reform, with the involvement of both government and professional interests in the preparation of proposals, more attention seems to have been paid to an examination of the likely outcomes of the change in the institutional structures and curricula than in the British case. Indeed, French governmental institutions led the way in a well publicized itemized analysis of the essential factors of teacher preparation: such as recruitment and selection of candidates, choice of teaching personnel, academic and educational preparation and location which preceded the introduction of the IUFMs (Bourdoncle and Louvet, 1991).

These factors were considered, monitored, and tested in pilot projects by civil servants, all of them qualified and experienced professionals, and others before being put in place. The professional management and siting of the new institutions was also carefully considered (*Ministère nationale de l'education*, 1993). Intensive practical teaching experience, both initial and in-service, was built in where it had not figured before, such as in the case of French *lycée* teachers, thus signifying an intention to make all the ingredients of teacher-preparation courses fit the overall purpose of reform. A similar involvement of professional and public opinion in the proposals for extensive school reform in Poland which are still underway serves the same purpose, which is to influence the course to be taken by the Polish reforms.

In England in the case of teacher education the policies made and put into practice in the 1980s and exemplified by the criteria set for training by the minister of education and administered through the Council for the Accreditation of Teacher Education (CATE) did not result so much from professional debate as from decisions made by Government acting on the recommendations of its nominated advisers. Since most, if not all of them, represent business and political interests, the recommendations are marked by a heavy commitment to market ideologies and by changes in the financing and validating of initial teacher training. The policies when published received much publicity, but the criticisms made by professionals did not deflect the course of reform, for example with regard to partnerships with HEIs, as argued in Part 1. No doubt controversy will continue to surround the Teacher Training Agency, which demonstrates the lesser degree of professional influence and involvement in the preparation of the reforms in England.

The Role of Higher Education and Schools in Training

The emphasis on free-market policies in the later 1980s was responsible for the accelerated speed and more radical character of the changes introduced in Britain compared with teacher-training reforms in mainland Europe, which are more likely to be characterized by the wish to modernize and improve standards. This is so despite the fact that in other sectors of education consumer-run schemes similar to Local Management of Schools (LMS) are being tried out in Poland for example. The early moves in the reform of teacher education in England and Wales can be conveniently traced to the publication of *Teaching Quality* (DES, 1983) which addressed teachers' needs predictably and largely in terms of two named components of professional preparation: subject knowledge and professional training. If the ensuing debate turned out to be diffuse and vague, this was because it coincided with the many other changes being introduced more or less at the same time, such as changes in the role of school governors, school finance and the curriculum.

The role of higher education in teacher preparation in France was affirmed by the explicit policy of raising the academic level of both components, knowledge of the teaching subject and professional preparation, thus spanning the two phases of teacher training. English reform has focused more exclusively on the second phase, with the demand for the improved teaching of the subject discipline, in the first phase coming predominantly from those seeking a return to an earlier golden age of excellence in subject knowledge. Here too, the progress of the Polish reforms parallels more those undertaken in France than in England and Wales.

Teacher education in France was extended to two years and in-service provision improved. In England the extended period for the one year PGCE route still comprises less than a calendar year while in-service provision has frequently been cut partly because of the new way of financing it at local level. In France the leading role of the HEIs working in conjunction with the IUFM is fully recognized, reinforced by the latest Bayrou changes which acknowledge the professional training task of the IUFM as part of the teacher-education centre set up in the twenty-eight *académies*, with the HEIs in the *académie* as the senior partner. However, although the French reform separates the more theoretical preparation received in the university from the more practical professional preparation part received in the IUFM itself, both have the status of higher education which is provided consecutively. After obtaining their *licence* the students spend, one year in the IUFM on further study of their subject discipline or year-group specialism including an introduction to its teaching methods plus the study of chosen theoretical educational subjects, followed by a year devoted entirely to practical experience, including extensive practical teaching and more methods work using the IUFM as a base. Details of course content agreed before the second wave of reform can be found in volume 13 of the journal *Recherche et Formation* (Baranger and Blais, 1993). Trainees can prepare for the competitive *concours* examinations in both institutions.

Current teacher preparation in Poland includes a new western model of civic and economic education and a concern with European integration. The professional preparation phase before the extensive practical teaching period itself has been placed more firmly in the hands of staff from HEIs. Improved in-service arrangements, a sector long believed to be lagging behind are located in former non-graduate teacher training schools, the *seminaria nauczycielskie* now being phased out, with the teaching done by university lecturers and graduate lecturing staff formerly employed in the *seminaria*. Non-graduate teachers can obtain a graduate qualification (*magisterium*), which normally takes five years to complete, in three years, at no expense to themselves if taken in state universities. Private HEIs, which are mushrooming particularly for the retraining and updating of language teachers do charge fees.

No immediate change is envisaged in the German model of teacher preparation, the professional side of which is received in a school with regular attendance at a local *Studienseminar*, where discussion of professional problems, methods as well as ethics, and the social context of teaching are part of the course. In many details the German pattern can be seen as the model for the articled teacher-training scheme which, as argued in Chapter 5, found a fleeting interest in England and Wales in the early 1990s.

The Higher Education Institution: Subject Discipline

While there are differences in detail in the duration and the actual timing and location of courses of study of the subject discipline the substantive parts of a future teacher's academic and personal education in the European union are received in HEIs. This study is not directly tied to a teaching career, however, the German pattern with its 'first state examination' taken at the end of a course of study probably has the closest link with the future career of teachers. The elective elements in education theory in Poland and France are fewer in number than in German HEIs and less binding. In the USA the first degree is not linked to the graduate's future career, since a further teaching degree, with extensive practical teaching is usually taken by those contemplating a career in education. More detailed comparisons are not helpful, but it must be pointed out that normally degrees awarded after three years of study in an HEI of a member state of the European union are mutually recognized, despite varieties in content.

The Professional Preparation Component

The professional preparation has always involved collaboration between the schools and the HEIs. What needs examining is the exact nature of this collaboration which has evolved over the years and in which professional preparation is acknowledged as at least a two-phase process, the academic (theoretical) and the professional (practical), with the school assuming more exclusive responsibility for the trainee during the period of practical preparation.

There are different ways of apportioning the work of the professional phases and their supervision. Indeed, with this in mind it is possible to posit a three-phase professional preparation model, which includes a probation period to follow the second phase which is best described as preparation for practice.

Practical Teaching

Short periods of observation-practical teaching which constitute part of the 'theoretical' phase which are received in an institution with the status of higher education though not necessarily a university, in some countries the result of recent reforms, are supervised largely by HEI staff. Again as a result of reforms this may not be so for much longer in England and Wales. More extended visits by school teachers to the HEIs are rare, although what was the Anglo-American practice of HEI-school staff exchange visits, now being lost in England, is finding interest in countries which have no previous experience of it, such as Austria (Kroath, 1989 and Altrichter and Posch, 1989).

During the second, practical phase of preparation the pattern varies again: in Germany contact between the two institutions may not amount to more than the schools receiving the new graduates after their first state examination to take up their practical work as *Studienreferendare* in a school teaching experience situation with no involvement on the part of the original HEIs. By contrast trainees in the IUFMs are still being 'educated' into the profession. In Poland 'inspection' visits can be made by HEI staff to schools to see the newly graduated teachers after their first phase of training.

IUFM staff, but not university lecturers, perform a similar, but much more extended, professional function in France. The American tradition has always been marked by close collaboration between schools and HEIs with the HEI the main partner providing the HEI supervision, a role which the advent of the Professional Development School (PDS) will enrich, as is discussed later. Experienced school teachers, often called mentors do the routine observations in all four countries. In Poland headteachers appoint new staff directly; their tenure is confirmed after a visit from the local education authority (*kuratorium*), in the absence of which the headteacher is the only validating authority.

In Germany there is both the 'second' (mainly practical) state examination which includes a subject dissertation and several teaching samples, for which trainee teachers prepare during the practical phase of training as well as a probationary period after that. The French *concours* examinations, are more substantial dissertations on topics to do with the teaching subject or the curriculum of the age group taught prepared for by trainees towards the end of their first and second years of training. They perform the function of selecting the candidates for induction into a higher professional grade. There is written work required in Poland and in England and Wales, as well as in Scotland. The British model was the much prized partnership described in Part 1, enabling a two-way traffic between school and HEI. It is the loss of the benefits of this why the reduction, or indeed abolition, of HEI involvement in teacher education in England and Wales is felt so strongly by all those upholding its role in professional preparation.

The extended practice is the period when the trainees are making a gradual start with real classroom teaching supervised in the main by experienced school teachers working both inside and outside the practice school, in mainland Europe with additional visits from ministry inspectors or advisors. In England and Wales until the arrival of the Teacher Training Agency (TTA) the period of extended professional teaching practice was traditionally supervised by experienced teachers assisted by HEI staff. As already mentioned in mainland Europe and America there is the additional phase of probation.

In England and Wales this extended teaching practice period, during which trainees are also required to produce written work, will most likely be the only period of closely monitored and supervised experience before the teachers are appointed to a full-time post. This feature, together with the virtual absence of an education component in the academic education phase, which, in England in any case, is generally not regarded as an integral part of teacher preparation, except insofar as it provides an education in the subject discipline, as well as the absence of probation, distinguish English practice most markedly from its mainland European equivalent.

The difference between English and continental practice is due to the way English and Welsh universities are involved in professional training where the demarcation lines between what is the more 'theoretical' professional (including academic and personal) preparation and what constitutes full professional practice are less clearly drawn, and where newly qualified teachers take over as fully operating practitioners when they start their first job. In keeping with the more 'liberal education' tradition universities in mainland Europe usually steer clear of much professional involvement, especially so in Germany (Tournier, 1993), though, as mentioned, they do so after providing the 'theoretical' professional (academic and personal) education in the first phase.

Comparativists are often surprised by the short duration of the period of teaching practice received by trainee teachers in Poland, Germany and France which varies in length from a few days to a few weeks, though there may be more than one such period. What is not taken into account is that this is the practice period during the more academic, that is the first phase of preparation. This phase is followed by a period of supervised teaching practice, which may extend for as long as three years, with the trainee teaching a reduced timetable. In addition all new teachers have to undergo a period of probation during which they are further supervised and monitored by the school principal, specialist ministry inspectors, and, as in Poland, the local authority (*kuratorium*) advisers. In England and Wales this is another job for the school supervisor and for OFSTED, with many English headteachers having little involvement with the new teachers in their schools, a role now usually assumed by the professional tutors with their responsibility for in-service education.

Theory

In mainland Europe the theoretical teaching provided by the HEIs has traditionally been more 'abstract', less 'applied professional' that is, in strictly academic terms. This distinction can be seen in the gamut of university-based education-centred and child-centred education theory courses on offer, which is rare in England and Wales but not in Scotland. Especially the German model can be illustrated by the long lists of courses mentioned by Kron (1988) which names fifteen educational study topics as options for the first state examination, each of which is capable of further subdivision.

Both kinds of theory are accepted as necessary for teachers. However child-centred courses have always been to the fore especially in the preparation of primary teachers reflected in the the emphasis given to child development in methods (didactics) courses. This is still seen in the names given to education faculties in many European universities: pedagogy and psychology in Warsaw for example and their concern with the preparation of teachers in primary and special education. The more subject-orientated preparation of secondary teachers is linked with special subject-specific courses which may be useful to the teacher, such as *kultura języka*, in Warsaw and Białystok, which can best be rendered as language awareness, or literature as perceived by children, and which are on offer in the appropriate subject discipline departments. Again, there are more such options in German universities, some of which can also be studied with a more practical emphasis in the second phase of preparation.

Whether teachers need to study sociology or history of education is, of course, one of the more hotly debated topics in the current English reforms, where the relationship between the theoretical and the practical parts of training has perhaps become the subject of more discussion than in Europe. There had been many debates on the respective roles of theory and practice, variously called 'theory into practice', 'theory out of practice', and other formulations in teacher-preparation courses but these did not become matters of public concern until the debate between Hirst and Simon discussed in Chapter 2. The further reduction in the education-theory component in teacher-training courses in England and Wales, the result of reform, with the term 'theory' being used pejoratively, is bound to accentuate the difference between teacher preparation in England and Wales and the other countries compared.

There are other reasons accounting for the policy in England. One may be the considerably shorter preparation period available in Britain compared with the continent, already referred to, and which includes the extended teaching practice. In mainland Europe the theory subjects affected are principally what the Germans call: *Politologie* and courses in sociology and history of education and comparative education. They represent theory as 'education and society' rather than theory as 'education and teaching'. The former set ('education and society') is already widely available as an option during the academic and personal phase of teacher preparation. Educational psychology and subject methods, which also appear in the first, the HEI phase (Kron, 1993), are studied in more detail and with an added professional emphasis during the practical training period of phase 2.

The false dichotomy between theory and practice in teacher preparation in England and Wales has been exacerbated by the adversarial way of introducing the reforms, dividing the two phases of preparation and the location of training. The two are complementary and it is important to see them in this light: the university contributes to disciplined ways of knowing, while the expertise of the school is based on custom, tradition and daily practice inside particular school cultures. (see Whitford in Darling-Hammond, 1994) A form of partnership is the best guarantee for successful teacher preparation.

European mainland practice has always accorded a place to theory in teacher preparation courses, specifying the number of teaching hours available to the different categories of teachers. In Frankfurt (the Goethe University) the course for future *Realschullehrer* provides for forty semester hours of education studies compared with only twenty for future teachers in the selective *Gymnasium*. The ratio is inverted in the case of subject methods, with 128 hours for the latter and only sixty-four for the former. The hours allocated for the different subject specialisms in the IUFM Bretagne show even greater disparity, however theory is studied in mixed groups of future *professeurs des écoles* and *professeurs des collèges* and *des lycées*.

In Germany the difference in the academic titles of *Diplom Padagoge* or *Magister* (Master of Education) as opposed to the first state examination in education, which is also found in the university study phase of most other professions, clearly designates the academic specialist as distinct from the civil servant professional teacher. By the same token, unlike school teachers, German university professors are not civil servants. Scottish universities which traditionally offer education courses as an academic discipline appear more 'continental' in this respect than most English and Welsh ones.

Indeed, there is a strong European element in all teacher education courses in Scotland, which cannot be dismissed as mere theory. Writing in *Working as a Teacher in Scotland* (Peck and Sutherland, 1991), the authors comment:

> In some ways Scotland has been ahead of its southern neighbour insofar as European developments are concerned. This derives partly at least from the existence of the General Teaching Council which is the focal point for the profession in Scotland . . .

> As a watchdog in matters of professional training the Council has been actively encouraging the training institutions to incorporate a European dimension strand/module in their pre-service training course . . .

> The Council will in time seek evidence from the training institutions of such developments when accrediting and reviewing courses of pre-service training.

Increasingly, Scotland emerges as another area of the European union from which current British government policies are separating teachers who have received their initial preparation in England and Wales.

Partnership

The question whose role, that of the HEI or that of the school, is the more important, has a meaning only if a professional partnership can be said to exist at all. In the United States the HEIs continue their partnership links with schools because the schools continue to function alongside the universities in a professional preparation process which consists of two linked experiences, both of which insist on their full professionalism (Cremin and Judge, 1982; Gumbert, 1990). The concept of the Professional Development School (PDS) which includes the use of training schools well equipped and prepared for the purpose capable of providing practical experience for a large number of well educated graduate trainees, could only arise in a situation where the professional status of all teachers is high and kept in debate. The PDSs will receive graduates for their mainly practical training (phase 2) with at least one academic degree, which as well as providing a good grounding in a subject discipline had given them an introduction to educational theory also. With all of the practical preparation side being left to the PDS (Holmes Group, 1986 and 1990), but without the total break between the two phases characteristic of Germany, they are well placed to be seen as providers of the 'clinical' period following the students' 'medical' study at university.

The PDS scheme has been in progress for nearly ten years with over 100 initiatives identified throughout the United States, but especially so in Michigan, Minnesota and Massachusetts, where the PDSs have become 'institutionalized' as part of the infrastructure for building a strong education system through basic aid allocations in the same way as other integral parts of the system (Darling-Hammond, 1994).

The PDS system came into being in order to introduce a more efficient system of teacher preparation. Unlike the English reforms it has been conceived to cater for the two phases of teacher training. This means that the PDSs work in collaboration with the HEIs, and under the best of auspices. A state evaluation of the 'alternative certification' programme carried out in Los Angeles which compared several different kinds of trainees, found the group who had enrolled in a regular university teacher-education programme while still receiving state-funded mentor support providing them with assistance in their first year of teaching, far outscored any of the other teachers trained exclusively in the HEIs or those trained in school summer programmes (school-based) in classroom effectiveness (Wright, *et al.*, 1987).

When Linda Darling-Hammond (1994, op.cit.) in fact suggests that:

> combining the knowledge-base built in the academy with the knowledge derived in close interactions with children, parents and colleagues . . . is a critical linchpin in developing teachers who can create learner- and learning-centered schools. (Darling-Hammond, 1994)

she is thinking of the PDSs and HEIs working together. Certainly in the United States the debate about the role of theory delivered by the HEIs and the professional status of the training school used for practice continues, as a stimulus to improving teacher preparation, made possible precisely because of the close links between the two sides. It is in this form of collaboration which recognizes the contribution made by each of the partners that a nucleus of a 'theory of teacher education', not a new concept having made the rounds in England and Wales in the 1970s, can be located.

The new institutions in mainland Europe, especially the IUFMs in France, insist on a close link between the HEIs and themselves, theory and practice in partnership. Regrets have been expressed by distinguished educationists like Gilles Ferry of Nanterre (Paris X) that the Bayrou reforms have shifted the emphasis in training, especially for the *lycée* teachers, more towards the subject discipline, a situation aggravated by the fact that trainees have to spend much of their time in the first year preparing a subject-orientated *concours* . .

The School Location

In Part 1 we have discussed the distinctive role of the school in teacher education as provider of an 'in depth' professional preparation, concentrating on practice and the purely professional aspects of training. The American evidence quoted above emphasizes the distinct cultural tradition of the school and its role in educating the teacher. The PDS model can have an important place in teacher preparation only if the experience they provide follows the theoretical study acquired in the HEI. Indeed, only in such a scenario the medical parallel of clinical training which has received much criticism in England can hold good. The reason why the PDS concept received the somewhat hostile reception in some quarters in Britain was because it was associated with Government plans for largely reducing, if not altogether eliminating, the role played by HEIs in the second phase of teacher preparation.

For the partnership to work the schools, like the HEIs, have to be ready for their distinctive role in phase 2 if it is to be more than providing sustained practice. Adequately equipping the schools is only one part of the story. The thinking and working climates encountered in school also require change. Trainees are not to do things by themselves. Experienced teachers are not to keep their experience to themselves. There must be time for collaboration, a feature that Darling-Hammond found characteristic of the PDSs she observed. This collaboration, we would add, must involve not only the old and the new teachers, but the HEIs and the schools and the other agents involved in education which we listed in Chapter 1.

In the PDSs seen it was noted 'everyone was learning together'; it was not a case of 'experts mentoring apprentices', a situation we posited in Chapter 4 as a condition for a successful partnership to develop. School reform is not to be confined to financial independence, but must go further to change the schools so as to make it possible for collaboration to take place; change must include change of practice as well as adjustments on the parts of both school and HEI staff.

In England and Wales, with most of the professional preparation components coming under the day-to-day authority of the school staff responsible for teaching them in the professional practice school there is the danger that attitudes will harden and that divisions will be confirmed through lack of exposure to new experiences. The new situation in England and Wales will require a much clearer definition of the professional, as opposed to the financial roles of the Teacher Training Agency regarding the responsibilities and competences of the new teacher trainers. Much of this cannot be legislated for. How does one enjoin staff to be open to innovation and how to adapt to new practices?

Implications for Staffing

Developments in England and Wales have seen the emergence of the 'mentors', a position well known in teacher education in other countries. Mentors work in conjunction with other school staff or local inspectors and specialists, indeed also HEI staffs, concerned with the teacher in training. In what is the longest established model, the German mentor is assisted by the subject adviser in the *Studienseminar*, the latter usually a practising specialist school teacher with a wider experience. As a permanent senior practising school teacher in the trainees' practice school the mentor directs their practical work which consists of observation, practical teaching of a limited number of lessons, discussion in school and in the *Studienseminar*. The subject adviser, the *Fachleiter*, a teacher in another school, who unlike the mentor, is attached to the *Studienseminar* is the acknowledged subject expert in charge of the trainee. There is no question of the work being entrusted to young and relatively inexperienced teachers.

In schools in England and Wales the professional tutor is an experienced teacher, usually in middle or senior management, often for most of the time no longer directly involved with subject teaching, who is involved in the training process by mediating between the HEI tutor, the mentor and the trainee. The general professional expertise seems to be gaining ascendance in England and Wales over subject specialism, which is in contrast to the situation obtaining in the other European countries discussed, where it is precisely the teaching of the subject discipline (or age group) which ensures the link between the school staff and the trainee. This too may have something to do with the growing depersonalization in England of the trainees' relationship with their mentors in England which is assuming the role of a commercial contract between the placing agency and the training school.

Attempts to define and agree the duties of a mentor in England and Wales have been the subject of recent literature (Wilkin, 1992; Wilkin and Sankey, 1994). Obviously, there are many different models in view of the wide range of schools and mentors used under the new school-based training regulations. We do not share the view (Hargreaves, 1994) that variety of practice is proof of poor preparation since it does not take account of the fact that the practical preparation of teachers is not an exact science. The greater uniformity in mainland Europe is due to the long period of existence of this particular teacher preparation model.

In France and Poland mentors can be both HEI and school staff. The German mentors are teachers, in the United States they can be both. As experienced teachers they take on the role of assisting younger colleagues, who in fact may themselves determine what help is needed. During the extended practice or probationary year the mentor may be asked to support the new practitioners should there be a clash of opinion as to their competence expressed by an inspector in the period before or at the final assessment. From the start a fully professional and collegiate relationship is aimed at. In the United States, where mentoring in the form of 'clinical supervision' is fashionable, the trainee often sets the agenda for supervisions, explicitly defining what aspects of teaching the mentor is to observe and comment on.

It is not surprising that the professional preparation of the trainers, which in many cases has not progressed much beyond the appointment of 'experienced' teachers should be the subject of new debates on both sides of the Atlantic.

Teaching is not the only profession to include an experiential element of personal commitment to work which cannot be put neatly into the categories of the two statutory phases of teacher preparation. We refer to the 'turning point' concept, an experience triggered off by a particular teaching situation in school in a third phase, the probational or indeed the early operational practical phase of preparation, which results in a change of behaviour on the part of the teacher relatively new to the job, but already in post (Kelchtermans, 1994). Schön's (1986) reference to a change in teaching after reflection, which emphasizes cognitive learning as being responsible without taking account of the way change affects the whole person of the teacher, is not to be confused with the above behavioural change. The factor of a personal input by teachers to their professional preparation must be emphasized in any debate on their education, which can be said really to begin once teachers have started on their first full teaching experience.

Assessment and Future Developments

The mutual recognition of teaching qualifications by member states of the European union will, despite Maastricht Article 126, impose a certain

degree of harmonization of teacher preparation. The cleanest break between the different phases of teacher preparation courses exists in Germany. With the implementation of current reforms, however, it is likely to emerge in another form in England and Wales. The break in Germany will remain one between theory, what can confidently be called a theoretical preparation period in the HEI, and professional practice in school. The English model will have the break between on the one hand what we called the academic and personal education which may be studied by the student in an HEI before any choice of career has been made, and professional preparation consisting of practice and what is left of theory, on the other, for which the HEIs have provided no input.

Any critique of the English situation has to recognize that in many schools professional tutors take their responsibilities towards newly qualified teachers very seriously. However the system has, so far at least, been a rather haphazard one, varying enormously from school to school, with the result that with the new way of INSET funding some freshly qualified teachers may receive little or no help at all.

It is possible to sum up this argument by predicting that the Anglo-American model of schools working in close partnership with HEIs in teacher preparation is unlikely to continue in England and Wales if the current reforms are completed according to plan. This is likely to be the case despite the fact that some recent English research showed the merits of school-based models of teacher education when linked with HEIs (Furlong *et al.*, 1988).

The continuing cash shortages have for a long time handicapped the development of education. They constitute a further threat to a successful outcome of the current reforms in initial teacher training. The principal aim of the 1994 legislation for teacher preparation in England and Wales was to create a new way of funding this sector of education. Paying the schools direct for the students trained is one way of changing its character; reducing or abolishing the teaching of what we have called 'education and society' theory is another. Whether this is likely to make the sector more attractive in economic terms, or more efficient by eliminating what some view as irrelevant contents, it is too early to say. Many reactions have been critical. At the 1994 British Association of Teachers and Researchers in Overseas Education (BATROE) conference held at the London Institute of Education views were expressed that such change virtually means exchanging a professional academic education for a form of apprenticeship training for all new teachers. It will reduce teacher training to a training in skills and turn the teacher trainers into technicians, with implications for classroom research, driving it in separate sociological and historical or teaching subject directions, the latter without the classroom research support.

We ought to add our disquiet about the payment situation. There is no similar extra financial reward, known to us, for providing teacher

education accruing to the individual school in other countries in mainland Europe, although obviously teacher supervisors and mentors are rewarded in various ways; time release being the most common. In England the money per trainee paid directly to the school is supposed to go to towards compensating the school for the extra time demands made upon the staff. However, it is often used for other purposes, for example enabling new furniture to be bought.

More details of the new financial arrangements for teacher preparation in England and Wales were given earlier in Part I. What is likely is that the unique market approach to education may prove another barrier between British practice and that in mainland Europe.

Innovation and Control in Teacher Education

Curriculum innovation and development is a particularly complex and sensitive matter within the parameters of state responsibility for compulsory schooling, including teacher preparation. What are the exact roles of government agencies, professional associations, business and industrial interests, and the general public?

The civil servant's role is to advise and to be consulted. The quality of the consultation itself depends on the competence and the seniority of those involved. The position of other parties in education depends on the status of their associations or the acknowledgment of their right to be involved and the degree of professional accountability expected. In the last twenty years or so this involvement has increased everywhere.

Governments are overly responsible for the institutional structures of compulsory education. Changing the status of polytechnics in England and Wales to that of universities was not a simple decision affecting their prestige, but had more to do with the administrative and fiscal policies of the government in power, regarding the financial independence and local-authority control of other tertiary-level institutions, as part of a policy to reduce the influence of local government of education (Strowbridge, 1994). Again the market element predominates contrary to the more professional concerns which seem to surround change being discussed elsewhere, such as in the mooted widening of the involvement of German universities in professional preparation.

In curriculum decisions governments' overt roles are less clear, since more than in the first category of polices much of the detail, despite leaks, is hidden by the work of commissions, committees and by government consultation. The introduction of the National Curriculum in England and Wales and the revisions dispelled the popular notion that teachers enjoy an absolute freedom to teach what they want. As against that, in France teachers will be directly asked for their opinion on the proposed changes in school education, as reported in a long interview article in *Le Monde* of 10 May 1994.

The German model of teacher preparation provides a unique exam-ple; its general structures and procedures have been in existence for almost two hundred years. The first phase, Higher Education is fully autono-mous, while school and professional education is more directly controlled by government agencies. This ensures that individual HEIs work to their own briefs. The situation in Poland is similar to that in Germany. In England the situation has been less clear-cut precisely because of the pro-fessional element being taught in the HEIs.

In the second phase there is more interdependence. In Germany the *Studienseminare*, in France the *académies* and, through the universities, the IUFMs in respect of teacher preparation have to act in accordance with government guidelines and are subject to control. There is considerable local government input in Poland. What does not happen, is that innova-tions are sprung on institutions at short notice, as has been the recent experience in England.

In Europe in the case of universities, which are mainly state-financed, the principle of government control requires them to submit course plans and the names of teachers and examiners who will teach them to the Ministry. It is extremely rare for any major intervention or changes to be made. Thus, those teaching and examining the courses, are deemed to have been approved by the minister to do so. Professional teacher-training in-stitutions ranking below the universities in this respect will have their in-dependence in the matter of teaching syllabuses and materials curtailed in proportion. This is in accordance with the constitutional principle of state control of education, which has been accepted in England and Wales also.

State supervision will apply to the programmes of study of the *Studienseminare*, and their equivalents in other countries. The one phase system of teacher education in Oldenburg presents its own problems. In the case of professional preparation which is carried out in the *Studien-seminare* and schools the curriculum proposals come from the relevant ministries in the first place. Compared with the autonomy of the HEIs, the process is reversed, with state or local administration in control of the contents taught and with the teachers and administrators consulted. Since all parties involved are civil servants the hierarchical principle of partici-pation determines much of the consultation processes. The involvement of non-professional lay persons, as in parent–teacher associations whose members may be civil servants but who in these instances do not act in this role, adds to the web of procedures.

The difficulty of crossing demarcation lines is a fact not easily under-stood by British and American (mainly) HEI teachers, brought up on the partnership principle, who wish to embark on classroom research with school teachers whom they find operating in a different sector of respons-ibility, where HEI staff may not be readily admitted.

There is finally the involvement of teachers' unions. The French unions have been particularly active in educational reform and fully consulted. In

Germany, the more elitist of the two major professional associations of teachers and university teachers, the *Philologenverband*, was opposed to plans made in the 1970s to give equal status to all teachers in Germany; a situation still not fully resolved. The professional comments of the British unions in response to the initial training reforms have been mentioned in Part 1, their effect no more successful than that of many others. The National Association of Head Teachers and the European Secondary Heads Association have made their influence felt with their recent criticism of teacher education in Europe. In Poland unions are in the process of re-establishing themselves after the period of communist rule.

The principle of local employer control to be found in the United States has more similarity with the situation developing in England and Wales. As against that, however, the professional voices as well as the role of the variety of affinity and interest groups are particularly strong in America. Scottish teachers, while not civil servants, are protected by their unions as well as by the General Teaching Council (GTC) an important agent in forming general educational opinion its role helped by being structured on an affinity with the Medical Council (BMA).

In England and Wales the universities' involvement in at least some parts of professional preparation is seen in the award of the BEd and similar degrees and especially of the PGCE. This is also the case in Scotland, though there these qualifications are subject to validation by the GTC. In England and Wales, the professional preparation of teachers, while provided in HEIs, is subject to validation by OFSTED, a function which in mainland Europe is performed by government in conjunction with the training agents. In England and Wales the Secretary of State must approve the validation, that is he accredits it if it is to lead to the award of Qualified Teacher Status. In Europe professional approval is given by the somewhat simpler expedient of a nod from the appropriate senior authority, a civil servant who is a professional expert. Professional associations, the Churches in the case of teachers of religious education, and teachers' unions are all more likely to be consulted in the validation process.

Powers held by ministers and their nominees manning the consultative and administering bodies, in Britain meanwhile many of them quangos, can overrule professional opinion. Though the seat of ultimate responsibility for education in most countries, including Britain, lies with the education minister the concentration of power in Britain, because the authority of local education authorities is on the wane, is stronger than with education ministers elsewhere.

With the likely diminution, or indeed the complete withdrawal, of the role of HEIs in initial teacher training in England and Wales, linked with the absence of a teaching council, the role of central government and its newly created agencies, including OFSTED, in imposing its own solutions is likely to continue to grow.

Consideration has repeatedly been given to the creation of a teaching council for England and Wales to provide for independent monitoring of the new procedures (Lawton 1992, Tomlinson, 1993, op.cit.). Given the experience ten years ago of the abolition by Government *diktat* of the Schools Council for Curriculum and Examinations which brought a large variety of educators to the centre of debate, even though its functions did not reach into the area of validating and approving teacher certification, this may be a rather remote prospect (Tulasiewicz and Taverner, 1989).

With teachers becoming responsible for the training of their colleagues, it might be assumed that, as is the case with the second state examination in Germany, the various parts of which are conducted in school by staff from the *Studienseminar* who in fact also teach in school, the same will happen with the school-based PGCE. The question to ask is how professionally reliable the new examiners will be, assuming that most of them for a long time to come will themselves have been trained under the old system.

Conclusion

The comparisons made have revealed similarities. These are surface only. Problems can only be fully appreciated in a detailed comparison of each element which uncovers the relationships which exist in education in action, with the roles of all the agents, the amount of human and material resources available as well as the impact of their confrontation in the teacher preparation situation. This would require a series of monographs. The quality of the consultation process determines the degree of democratic involvement of the participating parties. One is tempted to suggest that in the 'bureaucratic' system this is likely to be more formalized and thus, through the use of proper channels, perhaps more accessible.

In the German model of teacher preparation modifications have made use of the professional expertise of experts while being run according to a well tried bureaucratic pattern which has not changed.

In the period since CATE was established in 1984, teacher education in England and Wales will have exchanged an HEI supervised training pattern, also one with a long and distinguished history, for one devolved largely to the schools, themselves ill equipped and under growing pressure from other innovations, and put under unprecedented strong control from central government, as is the TTA.

What is not at all clear is what extra time the new teacher trainers will have at their disposal to look after their trainees and how much time they will have to become suitably experienced and qualified to assume the extra load of responsibility. We may remind ourselves that in ten years only some 100 PDSs have been identified in the whole of the United States.

What is truly most astonishing is that the most profound educational changes can be proposed and implemented with relatively little consultation with those most closely affected by them. This is the vital part of the background against which different systems of teacher preparation can be examined and compared.

Part 3

Educating the European Teacher

Chapter 8

Education and the European Union

Education and Training in the European Union

The eventual signing, in July 1993, of the Treaty on European Union (Maastricht), where Britain was one of the last signatories, opened up the possibilities of a new era of cooperation in education within Europe, hitherto unaddressed by the Single European Act of 1986. It is not surprising that, within months, it was followed by the Green Paper of the Commission of the European Communities on *The European Dimension of Education* of 29 September 1993. As the Green Paper itself makes clear, the deliberate exclusion of education from the 1956 Treaty of Rome meant that, until 1993, any attempted intervention by the European Community in this area of exclusive nation-state concern was a potential political minefield.

The original European Economic Community was created as a defence and economic union. Cooperation in the area of vocational training was principally intended to assist in economic development. Nevertheless, from the start, appeals were made to the common European heritage, a concern which can more readily be understood as educational, which was introduced in order to reinforce a feeling of unity among citizens of member states after the disastrous divisions caused by World War II, so as to bind them more closely together in their joint economic, and, in the days of the Cold War, defence pursuits.

Thus, stimulated by developments that had begun as early as the 1960s, such as the Janne report, to introduce joint aspects of education and training into the work and thinking of the Community, a Resolution of the Council and the Ministers of Education meeting within the Council on 9 February 1976, led to the creation of an education information network in the then European Community, EURYDICE, and a programme of study visits for education specialists, ARION. They provided an impetus to further joint exchanges and cooperation programmes in education which were a direct precursor of the ERASMUS Programme (created by the Council Decision of 15 June 1987) for the mobility of university students.

We note, however, that the European Centre for the Development of Vocational Training (CEDEFOP), begun on 10 February 1975, predated by a year the more exclusively educational initiatives, proof of the strongly vocational nature of European cooperation as seen by the Council at that time. There are, in fact, more industrially and vocationally linked Community initiatives than there are educational ones. The best examples are COMETT, a cooperation programme between universities and enterprises for education and training in technology, and PETRA, a community action Programme for the vocational training of young people and their preparation for adult and working life. This is a civic and employment preparation equivalent to the ERASMUS Programme, devised to promote student and staff mobility and cooperation between eligible higher-education institutions within the member states, now superseded by the SOCRATES Programme which we discuss later, which has in practice been particularly enthusiastically received.

Nevertheless, after the February 1976 Resolution, several promising pilot schemes, involving schools in addition to higher education, were easier to achieve. These culminated, in particular, in the Youth for Europe Programme which promoted youth exchanges for the age group 15 to 25 which did not fall either within mainstream education or vocational training. Other Programmes are more closely identified with particular school-curriculum subjects, such as LINGUA, a popular action Programme to promote modern foreign-language competence in the the European Community. Some curriculum-based initiatives have been taken up by individual member states, such as the 'Science Across Europe' Programme which began in the United Kingdom and now has a development team comprised of specialists from at least ten different countries.

Teacher Training and the RIF

Significantly, all the programmes, vocational or educational, outlined here have been initiated by the European Union Task Force IV (Human Resources: Education, Training and Youth). The fact that teacher education could be interpreted as training, indeed vocational training, meant that cooperation in this area, spanning both school and higher-education levels, was included. An example of the way in which cooperation at the level of Initial Teacher Training (ITT) could be achieved is to be seen in the very successful ERASMUS-supported initiative known as the RIF, *Réseau d'institutions de formation*, (Network of Training Institutions).

This 'network' began as a fairly informal mechanism for the exchange of information about work in teacher-training institutions across the member states of the European Community. It was established as a consequence of the realization that the exchange programme for students, with which ERASMUS was concerned, did not readily apply to the needs of student teachers. They were unable to be absent from their home institutions for the length of time stipulated for an ERASMUS grant, given the variety of systems of teacher education in member states, including such 'mundane' differences as those created by the very different duration of terms, or semesters, worked. A way had to be found of enabling exchanges, both of information and personnel, to take place at the level of student teachers and their trainers so as to accommodate their needs in view of their importance to the emerging 'New Europe'. The RIF, strongly supported by the Brussels officers, proved itself an effective means for this.

The RIF developed over a period of several years into a loosely linked pattern of 'subnetworks', sixteen in all in September 1993, each of which concentrated its energies on one aspect of teacher education. These include priority areas of concern such as, for example, a subnetwork on 'European Citizenship', one on a comparison of 'Educational and Training Systems', another on the 'European Dimension and the New Technologies', and further ones on 'Language and Intercultural Education', as well as others focused upon different areas of education in Europe. (A complete list of the RIF activities is given for reference purposes in Appendix 4.)

Whilst most of the RIF subnetworks published documents detailing their work which are their most tangible outcomes, other, less formal, outcomes were probably of even greater value. Each subnetwork consists of teacher trainers from a number of European-union countries, usually five or six, who meet each other frequently and who have gained experience of working together. Opportunities have also been made for bilateral exchanges to enable members of each subnetwork to visit and work in each other's institutions for short periods.

The difficulties which remained in enabling student exchanges were overcome in an imaginative and experimental way. This happened when some of the subnetworks organized seminars over a four-week period attended by two or three students from as many European-union countries as possible, staffed by teacher trainers drawn from the various institutions comprising the subnetwork. These included a series of seminars looking at the intercultural element in the European Dimension in Education, such as those held in Brussels in 1992 and in Barcelona in 1994. The work of the RIF, which proved remarkably cost-effective, is likely to continue with each subnetwork dividing and recruiting further institutions. The activities will be comprehensively reviewed in the light of proposals made by the new SOCRATES initiative, discussed in the following section of this chapter.

The importance of these programmes, which straddle the Act of European Union, lies in the fact that they have generated much common expertise and understanding across teacher-training institutions in member states and that they have pioneered models for bringing students into patterns of collaborative working. Sadly, the models for this work have involved only a minority of institutions, trainers and students, mainly in northern European countries.

SOCRATES and its Implications

Under Antonio Rubarti, the Vice-President of the European Commission in 1994, proposals have been made which are intended to streamline and rationalize the plurality of European union programmes. Effectively, by the start of 1995, ERASMUS, including the RIF, is to be subsumed within one of the two new EU initiatives, SOCRATES, an action programme for education, which will include new ERASMUS and LINGUA initiatives; the other, LEONARDO DA VINCI will implement European-union vocational-training policy.

The new programmes restate and reinforce former aims. For example, the three strands of LEONARDO take up the general modernizing, europeanizing and opportunity-increasing aims of previous activity. They include European-union support for:

- Strand 1: national measures to sustain the quality of member states' vocational preparation systems, arrangements and policies;
- Strand 2: measures to support innovative capacity in actions in the training market; and
- Strand 3: a network of accompanying measures promoting the European dimension.

These measures are intended to invigorate national-training institutions, through investment of monies, making them more European. They aim to facilitate exchanges, to introduce innovations and enable their transfer throughout the EU, to extend transnational cooperation in initial training systems, catering for:

- providers of training activities, including training bodies, firms, social partners, universities, and transnational language projects for firms; and
- socio-economic circles.

The last of these activities corresponds to the stated aim of the LINGUA Programme. Easy access and dissemination of results is to be achieved by a common framework of objectives for community action and a set of measures (Article 1), which are spelled out in detail in Annex 1 of the document (COM (93) 686 final), dated 21 December 1993, which foresee the need for facilitating integration into the labour market of improved initial vocational training and continuing training, facilitating access to it and encouraging mobility, stimulating cooperation on training and supporting exchanges of information and experience, through a variety of pilot projects, placements and surveys, with multiplier effect.

European networks, development of language knowledge, monitoring and assessment thus comprise the three strands to be financed by

European-union contributions. In keeping with the subsidiarity principle, which applies especially to education, the measures to be adopted, aiming at a 'progressive establishment of an open European vocational training and qualifications programme', are not initiated by the Commission but are projects intended to support and complement initiatives carried out by member states.

The proposal for the establishment of the community action programme in education, SOCRATES (COM (93) 708 final), dated 3 February 1994, pays even more respect to the independence of member states' national programmes and initiatives. This independence, which excludes any harmonization across educational systems, is in evidence in SOCRATES with its articles on subsidiarity (para: 26 ff.).

The economic aims in 'a changing Europe' take up the challenges faced by the European union and its member states respecting 'growth, competitiveness and employment', acknowledging that 'education and training policies should be . . . to support jobs', and that 'innovations . . . affecting . . . reform of school systems' are indicative of 'a cultural change'. Acknowledgment is made of what has been achieved to date by existing ERASMUS and LINGUA programmes and others, particularly in respect of their work in promoting mobility and exchanges. The European Parliament has adopted budgets under new headings including intercultural education and 'Europe at school' (Para: 18).

The Treaty on European Union made school initiatives of this nature possible by including, in addition to higher education, 'the full range of educational activities at all levels of teaching', arrived at by means of 'co-decision' (Article 126) and 'cooperation procedure' (Article 127). The specific objectives of community action in the field of education link it with:

- promoting economic and social cohesion;
- reinforcing the scientific and technological base;
- improving the knowledge and dissemination of the culture and histories of the European peoples; and
- encouraging operational synergy between the various activities of the Community.

SOCRATES presents its educational programme in three chapters which deal with: higher education; school education; and horizontal actions, the latter promoting language skills, open and distance education and learning, and exchange of information and experiences. SOCRATES, Chapter I (Higher Education), drawing on the experience of ERASMUS, LINGUA and other pilot projects designed to help fulfil the aim of higher-education initiatives, argues for inter-university cooperative activities by establishing large networks in higher education intended to culminate in a European Credit Transfer System (ECTS), initiated in 1989–90. The exclusion of any harmonization in education is somewhat mitigated by emphazising the link which exists between vocational training and education and includes 'the promotion of language skills'. The recognition of the work of teachers is acknowledged in continuing this proposal by the words, '. . . .may be combined with the training of teachers' (para: 6 of the SOCRATES programme). This clearly refers primarily to the training of teachers of European languages, but it is a useful start provided the parties affected are willing to engage in the collaboration made possible by the proposals.

Money is earmarked for developing a European dimension in courses to be followed by students in all phases of schooling. The objective is to strengthen the spirit of European citizenship, drawing on the cultural heritage of each member state, and to promote the knowledge of languages of the Community so as to achieve greater understanding and interaction. This would result in increasing mobility for students, enabling them to complete part of their studies in another member state and in promoting mobility of staff and intensive cooperation, developing use of technologies, intellectual mobility as well as encouraging academic recognition of diplomas and periods of study (Article 3 (Objectives) of the Decision of SOCRATES).

Increasing the range of languages offered is the particular concern of Article 6 (Objectives) which deals with cooperation with member states. Promotion of the European dimension in higher-education institutions (Action 1) is seen as evolving from transnational cooperation of every kind, the study of the economic, socio-political and cultural features of member states, the elements relating to European integration, the design of innovative joint programmes, and the establishment of European-union university networks for specific themes and disciplines together.

SOCRATES, Chapter II (School Education), encourages cooperation between schools at all phases of education to undertake activities of mutual European interest, and to update the skills of educational staff, to contribute to equal opportunities and also to help disadvantaged children, giving young people a sense of responsibility in an interdependent society, enabling them to familiarize themselves with the socio-economic and cultural situation in other member states, and to learn their languages. Networks for the exchange of information and experience at school level, improvement of teaching methods, the development of use of the new technologies, and the production of teaching materials will be promoted as in higher education.

Chapter III, (Horizontal Measures) envisages furthering activities in the areas of improving language skills, open and distance education and the use of the new technologies to increase the spread of information. The move is 'away from teaching staff working alone towards a more concerted approach' (para: 50). The promotion of language skills (Action 1) takes up the priorities of the LEONARDO programme for producing innovatory teaching methods and encouraging mobility of staff and students. The existing EURYDICE programme for exchanges of information and the ARION programme for study visits receive especial mention in this chapter.

The most innovative aspects of SOCRATES are the proposed 'institutional contracts' (for example, in languages or management courses), initially of a maximum three-year duration, which it is expected will result in the rationalization of cooperative activities, in economies of scale, and the involvement of all teaching staff in these activities. The European dimension aims to develop courses with a specific European content, for example on European-union law, and the development of transnational 'networks of researchers and teachers' to pursue common interests. This is envisaged at both higher and school education levels. The other promising area, in Chapter I, is the development of thematic networks across HEIs (Action 2), such as those concerned with language, technology and environment. The entire Chapter II of SOCRATES breaks new ground in proposing that, at school level, similar measures will be undertaken to bring together, again in thematic networks, pupils working on technology, linguistic and environmental projects, all of which are politically acceptable in curriculum terms and specifically mentioned in the 1993 Brussels Green Paper on *The European Dimension of Education* (op.cit.) resulting in wide opportunities for updating the skills of school staff. It is apparent that, laudable as these objectives are, and we have cited important portions of them *verbatim*, they are also rather diffuse, idealistic and grandiose, and that an infra-structure is needed to enable them to be put into effect.

Current developments, represented by such initiatives as the European Educational Regional Partnership, pioneered by Hertfordshire in England, suggest that the following considerations should apply:

- that the principle of subsidiarity is best applied when the level of decision-making is lower than that of the national member state, that is when it operates at a regional level. This means that, for example, in Hertfordshire and its ten associated regions in the rest of Europe, the administrators responsible have only to approach and persuade their immediate line managers, such as, in England, the Chief Education Officer, and do not need to go through national channels, in this case the Department for Education;
- that, in the interests of ensuring 'value for money', local initiatives, possibly supported through national organizations, such as, in England, the Central Bureau for Educational Visits and Exchanges or more specific research-funding bodies, such as the Leverhulme Trust, should provide initial funding. This may then be supplemented through EU funding when shown to be effective. This also implies the need for establishing mechanisms to ensure 'quality control' which may be best achieved through the

involvement of researchers and administrators from higher education and Local Education Authorities (LEAs), or their equivalent
in other European countries.

- that to ensure that such programmes should not be limited to the
experience of a single generation of pupils alone and so to guarantee that funding is justified, the institutions, schools, colleges, or
others, in which they are based, must be changed as a result of the
experience. This means that the programmes themselves become
an instrument for the in-service development of the teachers involved. They should also be designed so as to ensure a 'multiplier
effect', that is the experience should be transferable to other similar institutions. In much of the rest of Europe this may be achieved
by dissemination through teachers' centres, a feature pioneered in
England in the 1960s, now much reduced by the transfer of funds
from LEAs to individual schools as a consequence of local management of schools and the growth of grant-maintained schools.

SOCRATES and Teacher Preparation

Since, within the SOCRATES programme, PETRA, ERASMUS, RIF
and other activities, will continue, there is hope that teacher preparation
may be included in the proposals, although, apart from its being linked
with language work as stated above, there is no specific mention of it.
Falling as it does between the brief of the SOCRATES programme Chapters I and II, teacher preparation does not have its own distinctive identity
clearly established. As against this, however, it must be borne in mind
that the academic and personal education phase of teacher education, as
defined in the Introduction, takes place in HEIs, to which, of course, all
the proposed SOCRATES provisions outlined above apply. The challenge that now faces those who wish to work for more collaborative
patterns of teacher training and education in Europe is how to retain the
values of close personal contact and economy of scale while extending the
work more widely. It is necessary to make it available to all teacher trainers and students in the second, the professional preparation phase, of teacher
education within the European union.

A way forward towards collaboration in teacher education in Europe
presents itself in the recognition of qualifications. The directive, which
envisaged a general system of recognition of higher-education diplomas
awarded on completion of professional education and training, came into
force on 4 January 1991. This allows for the mutual recognition by all
member states of diplomas awarded for training for the same profession.
The vocational counterpart to the recognition of higher-education diplomas, that of a general system for the recognition of completed courses of
vocational training, came into force on 18 June 1994, following the 1992

Council Directive of the Education Committee of the Commission of the European Communities. Applying, as it does, to post-secondary level training in trade, industry, arts and crafts, as well as secondary-school level training programmes, it will inevitably affect all education, since the diplomas and certificates recognized are awarded at the end of the process of schooling. Although teacher preparation should also be mentioned in this context, the reason why it is not seems to reflect the wish not to trespass on member states' educational independence.

If teachers are to enjoy the same mobility as other professionals, teacher training will have to be included in the provisions of all three chapters of SOCRATES, and a place will have to be found for teachers in the programmes proposed. The danger is that individual member states will be able to invoke the principle of subsidiarity if they wish to opt out of some of them. It is revealing that while the English version of the SOCRATES programme, from which we quote, contains a long chapter on subsidiarity, the French equivalent document *Note d'information* dismisses this in a few brief sentences.

The SOCRATES and LEONARDO programmes have been debated and negotiated within the European Parliament and the Council of Ministers. At the time of writing the final version is expected in November 1994, and will not therefore be available until a joint decision has been reached. This means that the proposals are subject to modification. However, there has been little or no discussion either in the European Parliament or in the Council so far to suggest that any proposals, and this includes those that may affect teacher education, will be much changed from those listed above. The opinion on the proposal for a European Parliament and Council decision, enabling the Community action programme SOCRATES (94/C 217/06) of March 1994, endorses the proposal's programme, highlighting the 'subsidiarity and diversity' clauses. The realistic comment on the need for 'shorter placements abroad' (para: 2) which would help extend mobility over large 'networks for each discipline and faculty' is another realistic comment, as is the recognition that multilateral partnerships must consist of at least three institutions.

It is possible, therefore, to draw comfort from the expectation that the following proposals, which apply to all students, will apply equally to future teachers. These include:

- student mobility to undertake periods of study in another member state;
- joint development of initial or advanced curricula to facilitate academic recognition;
- mobility of staff, including administrative staff, for the purpose of transmitting instruction as an integral part of the curriculum in another member state; and
- intensive courses for students involving long periods of study

abroad; and the provision of teaching and learning materials centred on Europe.

The incorporation of the European dimension, including the learning
of languages, may also affect joint teacher-preparation programmes. The
final outcome, however, depends on each member state's policies in respect of teacher education, one of the most nationally localized sectors of
education. That is why it is stated that the European Community is there
to help ongoing projects and not to initiate action. The RIF has already
made plans for extending and streamlining its activities, in the evaluation
of curricula for specific disciplines, in the design of joint programmes, in
analysis and reflection on a specific area of studies and the development of
an information network for members.

It is tempting to read, in the words of the coordinator of one of the
RIF subnetworks (Ingelore Oomen Welke), promise for teacher education
in SOCRATES plans for 'updating the skills of educational staff (Chapter
II, Action 3), those responsible for the teaching, guidance and care of
pupils, to include . . . the development of teaching methods and materials,
especially those adding a European dimension' linked with the near cer-
tainty that the objectives and specific characteristics of the RIF will be
preserved under the SOCRATES proposals for the introduction of the
European dimension into the initial and in-service training of teachers. In
fact the RIF has been re-examining its subnetworks, looking for innovations, checking for overlaps and trying to involve more member states in
its networking activities.

It should be noted however that we have found no reference to the
development of a comparative methodology in considering the professional preparation of European teachers. This would be an essential component of European professional training which we address in Chapter 10.
The question is whether, and to what extent, national governments will
wish to be involved, if for no other reason than to make exchanges easier.
Official recognition of RIF activities is being sought through certification
and through human and financial support. Can English and Welsh academic and personal undergraduate education and professional teacher-training programmes, especially the latter phase which includes a complete
change of the location of training by shifting it largely to schools, in direct
contrast to continental policies, be made compatible with SOCRATES?

The European Dimension in Teacher Education

In the recommendations contained in the Green Paper on The European
Dimension of Education (op.cit.) there is more explicit mention of teacher
education than there is in SOCRATES. The recommendations single out
action at the Community level, including transnational educational projects,

emphasizing 'the training of teachers and others involved in education' and 'the promotion of innovation in teaching' (para: 23), acknowledging that teachers and their trainers are 'the main players in integrating the European dimension into the content and practice of education' (para: 28), despite the reservations provided through the principle of subsidiarity.

The important role played by teachers and their trainers is acknowledged in detail in Section III b of the Green Paper which sees teachers identifying new priorities and introducing the European dimension in their work 'to learn about the different aspects of Europe today and its construction for tomorrow'. Teachers are required to develop a European perspective alongside national and regional allegiances. This can be achieved by making use of, and passing on, the shared cultural heritage, and employing existing partnerships and networks to establish new teaching approaches, which 'overcome cultural and linguistic obstacles so as to develop multilingual and multicultural practices' (para: 29). The entire section III b of the Green Paper is specifically devoted to the training of teachers and others involved in education within the legal framework of Article 126 of the Treaty on European Union.

A problem, already hinted at in comments made about the diffuse nature of the earlier recommendations, is that the Green Paper does not admit the difficulties in defining what constitutes 'a European dimension', as opposed to bilateral, such as Anglo-French, schemes of cooperation. Neither does it show how teachers other than teachers of modern foreign languages, whose task has always been relatively easy to define, can be fully integrated. Section III e, ' Innovation in Teaching', which mentions sharing of problems and methodologies on particular themes, confines these to achieving 'economies of scale' and 'cooperation between research institutes and universities on educational issues', all of which is happening already. It also deals with 'the study of innovation and cooperation strategies in, and between, schools in different member states' as contributing to 'improvement in the quality of education' without listing the exact areas and nature of such cooperation; nor does it state exactly what is meant by 'quality'.

The SOCRATES proposals have to be read in conjunction with the Green Paper. The former does not explicitly name student teachers, but, in acknowledging the 'mobility of teaching staff for the purpose of providing instruction' (comment by Council of 18 July 1994 on Action 1), it leaves room for support to our proposals to work towards 'a European teacher'. In-service work has a better chance than initial training (Chapter II, Action 3) judging from the wording 'updating and improving skills of educational staff'.

Applying these recommendations, therefore, is not an easy task. The danger of trespassing on member states' national preserve of school curricula and timetables in any detail, since all intended activity must take place within the legal framework of Article 126, is real and may lead to failure. While there is a clear commitment to the means of improving communication, for example by promoting distance learning through multimedia systems (Section III d), innovation in teaching (Section III e), and the exchange of information and experience (Section III f), the exact educational element of the European dimension is difficult to discover, beyond that of contributing to European citizenship (Section II a), of passing on the cultural heritage (para: 29), or preparing young people for their integration into society and a better transition to working life (Section II c). Of these only the first is specifically European.

A European dimension component has to be supplied for each of the other recommendations and the advantages of introducing it considered and decided by individual member states. Better transition to working life is certainly desirable and will entail inculcating an open attitude to new working practices and to working with a set of foreign workmates. The wish for this will vary in the different member states; it is probably still a relatively low priority in Britain in most professions.

Potential Future Developments

The challenge is in devising programmes for teaching and teacher training. While there will be broad agreement on including knowledge of languages and familiarity with 'other cultural and professional environments' (para: 19), there is no precise curricular commitment to this by individual member states. Provision in England does not match that of Scotland, where modern European languages are taught in the later years of the primary school and where the European dimension, following General Teaching Council initiatives, is a recommended part of the school curriculum. Helping young people 'to move out into the world and to be able to master change' is little in evidence in British ministers' reluctance to make a firm commitment to 'change in Europe', endorsed in the Green Paper.

The failure to convincingly translate the lofty ideals of the Green Paper into concrete actions is likely to increase doubt amongst many Eurosceptics. Indeed, how to translate teaching the European dimension into quality education was a point made by Tim Boswell, education minister, in his written response of 2 December 1993 to the Green Paper. Even so, the potential of the 'value added', financial and experiential component (para: 9), to be provided by community action to agreed initiatives on syllabuses and curricula, such as those for European citizenship and a sense of responsibility in an interdependent society, are encouraging and are invited to be singled out by curriculum planners for the enlarged European union in each member state.

The perspectives having been delineated, it is up to the governments of member states to agree on action. Teachers are the obvious disseminators and initiators of any activity since, as we have seen, both articles 126 and 127 of the Treaty on European Union might also be applied to teacher education which should include a European element. We would argue, therefore, that as a consequence of the logic of the developments leading up to, and including, the Treaty on Union, all future teacher education in the Union should embrace three separate dimensions: European, national, and local, or regional, in order to educate the European teacher.

The Challenge of Union

In Chapter 10 we propose in more detail ways of enabling teachers in training in the European union to have a larger proportion of time devoted to developing their understanding of their role and professional practice as European teachers. All should have at least a minimum entitlement in this area. There will also be, varying between countries, a need for a national programme for teacher education, a minimum requirement, which acknowledges existing educational policies, such as the National Curriculum in England and Wales, devised by member states; and, finally, there is a need for teacher education to explore and utilize local needs and opportunities, to give a voice to minority interests, which is a distinctive area of European-union concern. While we subscribe to the European dimension aims of SOCRATES and the Green Paper they mainly consist of what might be called 'efficiency' clauses. The European dimension, in our view, must go beyond this in identifying a European teacher who is committed to the European ideal.

Speaking at a seminar for teacher educators, organized by ERASMUS, in Leuven in September 1993, Professor Hermans, a member of the European Parliament, stressed that:

> the diversity of national and regional educational systems constitutes the richness and one of the strongest points of Europe . . . to reach a higher quality and a better use of the existing resources and the available know-how. (Janssens and Loly-Smets 1994)

The desirability of a 'unity in diversity' model has similarly been advocated by Malcolm Stobart of the Council of Europe. The concept of intercultural education would include all three elements suggested above, thus adding up to a sense of 'a Europe still to come'. In order to achieve this, we envisage teachers who are being trained in Europe working towards a European element in their training to the extent of the minimum laid down by national legal requirements, such as, in France, those formulated in programmes approved by the Ministère de l'Éducation Nationale, or, in Scotland, by the professional guidelines of the General Teaching

Council. The mutual recognition of qualifications in Europe speeded up through the European Credit Transfer Scheme should be applied to teacher education as is already the case for undergraduate studies. As a precedent this would augur well for the time when teacher training is no longer confined to a student's country of origin.

Modern Linguists are already expected to spend a term of their training abroad, a scheme which is being extended at undergraduate levels to such other subject areas as environmental or civic education. Specific training in, for example intercultural education, may be gained by students being trained in an inner-city area and may depend upon local arrangements and student wishes. It could be experienced in more than one country. For such a pattern to work, the three dimensions, European, national and local, must not be isolated in separate compartments but there must be liaison between them. The initiatives of the vocational PETRA programme explicitly encourage the joint development of training modules for the training of trainers and 'support for placement in another member state' to 'enable trainers to use their experience in their day-to-day training practice'. (PETRA, 1993). On present evidence these opportunities seem still some time off in teacher training, despite the encouraging developments in enabling 'mobility of training staff for the purpose of providing instruction forming an integral part of the curriculum in another member state' (European Union: Common Position (EC) No/94, adopted by the Council on 18 July 1994: Action 1 A).

'Quality education' cannot be delivered by a workforce of teachers skilled exclusively in the technical aspects of their vocation and operating within the economy of the market-place. Such a need can only be fully met by a workforce prepared to work efficiently and in harmony in the changed multicultural society. Philosophers of education, from Aristotle onwards, have urged the need for education to develop the full range of human domains, including, alongside the intellectual, the physical, the practical, the emotional, the social and, in the widest sense, the spiritual. More recently distinguished educationalists in Europe, such as Gilles Ferry and Antoine de Peretti in France, or Derek Heater in England have interpreted this to argue for the inclusion in a European curriculum, besides communicative skills, the need for common values and for common concerns through peace and citizenship education initiatives. We argue for a European dimension, consisting of such obviously acceptable elements in the education of all teachers. In the PETRA programme, with its call for the 'development of a European dimension in initial vocational training' this seems to be in place already.

In fact, the European dimension in education, as defined in the May 1988 Resolution of the Council of Ministers, included a number of detailed aspects of common educational work long before the Maastricht Treaty had been signed. Indeed, there are some curriculum emphases missing from the 1993 Green Paper, in particular:

- promoting a sense of European identity;
- helping pupils and students acquire a view of Europe as a multi-cultural, multilingual community not forgetting that this includes their own nation state;
- enabling young people to acquire the necessary knowledge, experiences and the often forgotten skills (which go beyond those of knowing another language) to live and work in Europe comfortably but not uncritically;
- preparing people to take an active part in economic and social development, an education often obscured by the acquisition of facts about Europe; and
- furthering an awareness of European development, past and present, with 1992 marking only a stage in the progress.

We accept that the omission in the Green Paper of the very elements that a European teacher requires to work in the New Europe does not mean a cooling of enthusiasm, though it shows the influence of the more restrictive articles of the Treaty. Significantly there is also mention of 'ideals' and of the 'stage beyond 1992' in the National Curriculum Council's definition of the aims of the European Dimension (Tulasiewicz, 1993a) which, after this reference, are never again mentioned amongst the targets of the National Curriculum in England and Wales.

Towards a European Education

In view of what has been said, we propose that an adequate European education should include at least the following concerns:

- Living together — to include intercultural concerns; civic education, including the rights and duties of European citizens; and environmental education;
- Working together — to include professional and vocational skills necessary for the workplace, together with the capacity for 'getting on together', which entails communication skills, both linguistic and non-linguistic, together with information technology; and
- Playing together — to include using and respecting each other and the environment; aesthetic and cultural pursuits, including sport and physical education; and education for responsible leisure.

If these concerns are to be taught in schools, it is necessary that they be addressed also in teacher education. At present they do not, as constituted here, figure in day-to-day school-curriculum programmes in any European country. Nor do they figure as options in programmes for academic-degree courses in the older English universities. They are to some extent beginning to be introduced in courses taught in the former polytechnics in England and in multidisciplinary degree courses in the Netherlands, such as European studies combined with chemistry, or law combined with German. As reported in *The Times*, some engineering degree courses in Cambridge will in future include a European component.

Though they are not prominent in official teacher-preparation programmes, initiatives such as the RIF and SOCRATES are bringing them to the notice of educators. By way of contrast, in England and Wales the Council for the Accreditation of Teacher Education courses, (CATE), removed the explicit reference to Europe in the 1992 version of its criteria. Ecological concerns or information technology are often taught mainly for their scientific or technological skills, with little or no reminder of the European ideal they could serve.

The precise task of responding to the demands of the European dimension in education has been left to the governments of individual member states. Each of these will be interpreting these demands in different ways. In some cases there may be relatively little enthusiasm for new developments. The constant reiteration of the need for foreign-language teaching in schools in the Statement on The European Dimension in Education published by the then Department for Education and Science (DES, 1991a) is one example.

All the initiatives both European and national described in this chapter have operated primarily on the principle of mutual sharing of information and cooperation following the original 1976 Resolution. It is now necessary that they be translated into a cohesive action programme.

Chapter 9

The Schools in Europe after 1993

Introductory Comments

Some of the European union's initiatives to be developed in higher education, outlined in the previous chapter, eventually have to be, and in part, at least, are beginning to be, reflected in actual classroom practice in school education in the European Union. This lends a legitimacy to the teacher-training proposals we make and which are presented in Chapter 10.

International Multicultural Classroom Research

Our classroom proposals arise in part directly from the evidence of our own classroom observation and research in several European countries (Adams *et al.*, 1992), and in part from teachers' and pupils' responses to questionnaires on attitudes to Europe, such as that developed by Michael Evans in the Cambridge University Department of Education or in the European games published by the Federal Trust (McLaughlin, 1994). Several classroom initiatives were monitored by us for organizations such as the Central Bureau for Educational Visits and Exchanges and the United Kingdom Bureau for European Education.

Our own international research, beginning in 1990 and carried out over eighteen months, was concerned with intercultural education in selected classrooms in England, France and Germany. It revealed, at least in those areas of the three countries which were studied more closely, that there were very different attitudes to Europe in terms of *knowledge* about Europe and *attitudes* towards Europe on the part of both teachers and pupils. In general, we found that the Germans were perhaps the most knowledgeable, and the English least. However, our work in the London borough of Newham showed the high degree of European consciousness of many of the 'new European' members of the Asian community, who were often moving around the various European countries to visit their extended families. Indeed, many of the Asian pupils we spoke to were far more aware of other European countries and national customs than their peers were from a purely English background.

At the same time the research revealed generally positive attitudes by the young towards European integration. Though integration was by no means an easy concept for younger pupils to grasp who understood it in the sense of close contacts, such as those involving school twinning, it was encouraging to register their positive views about Europe and opportunities for employment. If, in the last two years, the enthusiasm we noticed then has diminished in all three of the countries visited, the reasons for this are less to do with alienation from the European union, as such, and more the result of the impact of recent waves of immigration into countries from outside the European union, coupled with worries about the economy and employment. These topics were especially raised by older pupils. The pressures resulting from the reunification of Germany have meant that the goodwill extended to minority groups is unfortunately much less widespread in that country than formerly.

There were many similarities to be observed in the treatment of minorities in the classroom in all three countries. We gathered evidence that minority pupils did not receive sufficient attention in having their own culture and language respected and supported in school, made the subject of the lesson for example, or indeed used as a vehicle of communication in parts of the lesson. Interestingly enough, again there seemed more sensitivity to such issues in England than in the other two countries investigated, observed, for example, in the presence of notices around the school in ethnic-minority languages, and in references to immigrants' customs and traditions in school assemblies, which might, in fact, be held bilingually. There has frequently developed a tradition of celebrating festivals such as Diwali alongside that of Advent and discussing the achievements of Mary Seacole alongside those of Florence Nightingale.

We deplore that, in recent years, there has been something of a renewed attack from the political 'right' on multicultural initiatives. The City of Birmingham was, for example, much criticized in the press in December 1993 for replacing its traditional Christmas lights at that time of the year with ones representative of the various 'Feasts of Lights' of its different ethnic communities. In Germany, some parents complained about too much attention being paid in class-time to Turkish and Kurdish children and their problems (Halstead, 1988 and Hamburger, 1991). We observed close relations between teachers and parents and the leaders of the local minority communities in England, with many parents regarding their children's teachers as counsellors when dealing with the authorities. This was supported by the practice of parents coming onto the school premises to collect their children at the end of the school day. Some good work of this kind was also observed in those schools in parts of Germany, where parents were encouraged to enter school premises. In Germany, too, use was made of ethnic languages in class to celebrate special occasions or festivities, which was criticized on occasion as taking away time which might have been spent on teaching the Germans German. Similar views have also been heard in Britain. These practices have much to do with the freedom of individual schools in organizing both curricular and extra-curricular activities, particularly easy in the more autonomous school structure in England and Wales.

It was only in France that there was a compulsory *Education dans la langue et culture d'origine* (ELCO) element which made it possible to have certain classes taught in Arabic, rather than in French, financed by the French government and attended also by some French children. In German schools there were many classes in Turkish for the children of Turkish guest workers but these, by contrast, were funded wholly by the Turkish government and attended only by the Turks. Neither Arabic nor Turkish are official European-union languages. According to a Brussels declaration of 1976, children whose mother tongue is one of the languages of the European union should have the opportunity, if they so wish, to have instruction provided in their mother tongue. However, the fact that this need not be adhered to if it causes undue expense may mean that, in practice, the opportunity for, say, a Turkish pupil to receive instruction through the medium of Turkish in Germany is often greater than that of a German pupil to receive instruction in German in France. This may be changed by the new Committee of the Regions (COR) arrangements.

In all three countries visited, the programmes of instruction were laid down by bodies external to the school. These might be national, as in the case of England, where the curriculum is determined by the Secretary of State, advised by the Schools Curriculum and Assessment Authority (SCAA), which has replaced the National Curriculum Council (NCC), with only minimal regional variation in the cases of Wales and Northern Ireland. In France, despite the myth of central control exercised by the Minister of Education, the individual *académies* (the regional bodies for the administration of education) have considerable freedom in curricular emphases, for example in the use of territorial languages, such as Corsican, for instructional purposes, and in the encouragement of a much broader spectrum of instruction in foreign languages. The German federal pattern enables each *Land* to have its own regional variety and responsibilities over curriculum content and educational structure. The consequence is that very different programmes of schooling were being followed in the three countries studied, with sufficient free time at the teachers' disposal to allow the possibility of introducing intercultural European syllabuses. We regret that there was little evidence of this opportunity being taken.

The evidence presented in the research suggested that the ethnic mix of classrooms would increase and that schools would have to absorb new immigrants from eastern Europe and the middle east, with the movement of populations within the European union itself continuing to increase. While education policy would necessarily remain the prerogative of individual member states, more common measures would need to be adopted, in particular the wider introduction of new approaches to language teaching and education in intercultural relations.

An important phenomenon revealed in our research was that the interaction we observed between schools was inevitably bilateral, with only a few initiatives involving pupils from three or more countries. Apart from the obvious logistical difficulties, it is, of course, difficult for young people to conceive of Europe as consisting of twelve or more countries.

The main purpose of foreign-language teaching in school is to establish communication with others using the target language. This helps to foster a link between the two countries concerned, to the exclusion of others, causing bilateral attitudes to flourish. As a further result 'Europe' may be identified exclusively with more 'cognitive' school subjects, such as history, geography, or the reading of literary texts, becoming less accessible to those pupils who feel more at ease in simple exchange, or twinning, activities, involving pupils in 'doing' rather than in 'studying' (Tulasiewicz, 1993a). Interestingly, in answers to questions put to young children such as: 'Are you European?', many English children denied this by saying that they were 'English'. In France, too, it was the other nationals who were regarded as 'Europeans'. It was noted that pupils felt more inclined to visit other countries than to receive foreign visitors in their own country — this was observed especially in Germany and Britain — with some countries, like Belgium, seen as decidedly more attractively 'European' than others. The links that can be established between two, or perhaps three, countries, therefore, must be conceived in such a way as to enable them to stand as a kind of proxy for the rest of the European union.

European Attitudes in Questionnaires

The questionnaires devised by Evans (an excerpt from which is given in Appendix 4) and by the Federal Trust explore not only school pupils' cognitive knowledge about Europe, but also their attitudes. By dividing them according to pupils' gender and ethnic background Evans' study goes beyond simple responses. General knowledge quizzes have been applied to teachers in training as well as pupils for some years, especially in modern foreign-language courses. What makes Evans' questionnaire important is that it does not ask only factual questions, but seeks to tease out through which school subjects (including physical education alongside English) the biggest contribution to pupils' first and second-hand knowledge about, and attitudes towards, Europe was made.

In addition to cognitive and affective knowledge about Europe pupils also need to acquire the skills that will enable them to behave as Europeans rather than as tourists. This can be approached through a variety of subject areas, such as the cooking of meals from different European countries in food-technology lessons, the reading of maps in applied geography, and the ability to use databases so as to obtain air or other travel information. In this connection the United Kingdom Centre for European Education (UKCEE) in partnership with the Central Bureau for Educational Visits and Exchanges, both parts of the British Council, have for some years been administering a European school competition, which has unfortunately only been taken up by a minority of institutions, largely because of pressures on teachers' time. We hope that, as a consequence of the Dearing (1993) proposals for the freeing of 20 to 40 per cent of curriculum time for schools in England and Wales to allocate according to their priorities, more opportunity will be taken to engage in such initiatives, which may in fact be financed through the European union. Recent statements by the Secondary Heads Association suggest that, in spite of the intentions behind the spirit of Dearing, even the new slimmer curriculum which is to be introduced in September 1995, will continue to take up most of the school week.

Finding a European Curriculum

A curriculum with a wider European consciousness can be found in some schools but is not yet extensively practised. Since, in each country, the formal period of schooling terminates in national leaving certificates, which do not allow for the easy introduction of additional European material, ways of establishing a school-leaving certificate which would enable this should be explored. In fact, with the specific requirements of teacher education in Europe in mind, there is an increasing need for a common outcome of secondary education before entry to higher education, an action encouraged by the proposals for mutual recognition of vocational qualifications found in Chapter 1 of the LEONARDO DA VINCI programme. In particular, so far as England and Wales are concerned, the maintenance of Advanced Level examinations, as a kind of 'gold standard' of educational excellence, referred to once again, this time by Gillian Shephard, Secretary of State for Education, on the occasion of one of her first interviews on taking office in July 1994, puts England and Wales out of step with the rest of Europe. Acknowledging the desirability of change, the move towards a broader base for the final years of school education, both up to and beyond the period of compulsory schooling at 16, has much to recommend it. The International Baccalaureate (IB) is one such examination, which can be taken after studying the normal national curriculum, with additional European elements, like extra modern languages or periods of European history. The flexibility of an IB-like package has been praised by the Labour opposition, while the Advanced Level has continued to attract criticism during 1994.

In considering pre-entry qualifications for prospective teachers there is a considerable difference in England and Wales between the somewhat arbitrary demand for qualifications at General Certificate of Education (GCSE), level C, or above, specifying English and mathematics for all teachers, irrespective of the subject they are going to teach, and the requirement, such as that found in the IB, of a 'package deal' of subjects ensuring a broad coverage, which is common in all other European countries, including, of course, Scotland with its Higher Leaving Certificate.

Although, in England and Wales, the IB is still a minority examination, it is one that evidence shows to be on the increase as was shown in an article in the *Guardian Education* on 11 May 1993 where it was stated that, at that time, about thirty-one British institutions, about half of them independent or international schools, were offering the IB. With more sixth-form and further-education colleges moving in this direction this number seems likely to grow.

This is also the case in countries outside Europe. Nevertheless, the IB still has to find a wider following in the face of established national-educational systems with their own school-leaving certificates. So strongly entrenched, however, are the national curricula and certifications that there is a constant plea to open up new 'national' schools in foreign countries, such as French and German schools in England, or 'American' international schools all over Europe. It is noteworthy that these generally exist at the more academic, such as the *lycée*, levels of education.

The IB is very European. Many of the Brussels Eurocrats have themselves attended schools leading to this qualification, and its wider adoption should improve the opportunities for mobility, despite resistance from those who continue to advocate existing nationally based certificates. This move has attracted followers amongst Eurosceptics in several European member states.

It is encouraging that the European Union will recognize a range of national educational qualifications in different member states as starting points for entry into higher education, including teachers' colleges, even if individual HEIs may require specific additional paper qualifications for entrants to particular courses. This is unique to the European Union in there being a range of different school-leaving qualifications mutually recognized in sixteen different countries, all of which have their own traditions of educational practice. This is far from being the case, for example, in the United States where different states may interpret different qualifications very narrowly, including the mutual recognition of teaching qualifications.

A European Curriculum Tradition

A European education of a sort already exists; for example in the broad similarity of syllabus content in such subjects as mathematics and the mother tongue, although the percentage of time allocated to national history and geography and the length of time for their compulsory study may differ. What is needed is an intention to identify common European curriculum objectives, such as might be represented by equal opportunities and the processes of bringing people together. In *Britain and a Single*

Market Europe, McLean (1990) defines three traditions of European education: encyclopaedic, naturalist, and humanist. The first two he sees as predominant in continental Europe, whilst the last he describes as peripheral, mainly located in the British Isles, including Ireland, and in Greece. In a closely argued analysis he shows how national-education systems are rooted in one of these different traditions of thinking and how this leads national characteristics in school curricula to predominate.

Ironically national priorities are invoked even by those who appear wholeheartedly devoted to the European cause. This is often achieved by their tendency to think in terms of the past, of the unity that once was Europe, for example the Europe of Charlemagne, that of the Holy Roman Empire, or of Napoleon. It may also be recognized in the attention paid to medieval history in national school curricula.

What would be more important as a school subject is contemporary history, which would explore the future of a united Europe through a socio-political and cultural analysis of the past. In this context it may be noted that a former British Secretary of State, defined history as anything that had happened more than twenty years previously; anything more recent than that was not so much as history as 'current affairs', a decision with implications for an accompanying diminution in the number of lessons available. The new National Curriculum proposals tend to lay particular emphasis on British national history (Dearing, 1994b) and the accumulation of factual knowledge, leaving little space for the discussion of contemporary European problems.

It had been decided in 1993 (Dearing, 1993) that, in the new National Curriculum, history and geography would cease to be compulsory subjects beyond the age of 14, a further example of increasing narrowness and insularity, happily not found in any of the other member states of the European union. The proposed geography syllabus does at least contain a specific reference to the European union in its programme of study for Key Stage 3 (Dearing, 1994b), that is for 14-year-old pupils, though its study is not compulsory. It was further conceded in 1993 (Dearing, op.cit.) that modern foreign languages for all up to the age of 16 could be replaced by 'short courses', which, in the UK, tend to be seen solely as a means of affording better job opportunities in Europe. With the intention that the new National Curriculum in England and Wales will remain intact until the end of the century, there is a serious danger that the 'slimmed down' curriculum will be even more inadequate than the previous version in providing a European curriculum.

To overcome any lingering separate European traditions of education, we should be encouraging throughout the European union a curriculum commitment to promote a modern single Europe. This could be furthered by studying texts in translation from across the European continent to help pupils appreciate the cultural achievements of other countries, or by developing European-wide initiatives, such as the European atlas, being prepared by a working team in the Council of Europe, intended to produce non-ethnocentric materials to supplement national geographical teaching resources. Environmental protection initiatives in the curriculum should emphasize cooperative action in addition to learning about the physical composition of one's surroundings. Language-awareness programmes must be designed to develop linguistic sensitivity, in addition to linguistic skills, and to encourage awareness that communication in cooperation promotes changes of attitude and motivation. A further contribution here would be the development of programmes in European citizenship, such as those established in France, to supplement the well-established tradition of education in French citizenship which goes back to the days of Napoleon. In England, in 1990 the Report of the Speakers' Commission on Citizenship (House of Commons, 1990) argued for a widening of citizenship education in schools but it seems unlikely this will survive in a meaningful shape the changes in the National Curriculum.

The European dimension was suggested as a common curriculum element in schools of the European Community. With member states autonomous in matters of education there was difficulty over negotiating an agreed version and the kind of pedagogical direction it should have. The 24 May 1988 Resolution of the Council of the European Communities (88/c 177/02) required member states to set out policies for incorporating this dimension in education. The Committee of Ministers of the Council of Europe had prompted a similar initiative in 1983 (R (8) 4). The DES did not respond until February 1991. Responses from other countries were lukewarm, with the Benelux states and Portugal predictably the most enthusiastic. A formal publication of the DES, *Statement on the European Dimension in Education* (DES, 1992) accommodated the European dimension as a cross-curricular element to be integrated into the National Curriculum. In the event the dimension died an obscure death, when the National Curriculum Council failed to produce guidelines for it. The subsequent revisions of the National Curriculum, aimed at 'slimming down' the curriculum, found no room for any of the other cross-curricular elements.

The European dimension continues in the case of extra-curricular exchanges, school twinnings and similar initiatives. The agreed Community definition of the European dimension is given in the previous chapter where it is compared with other definitions of the European dimension in education. Voluntary school activities are more widely practised in some countries than others; however only one European-union country so far has converted it into an integrated part of the school curriculum. In England and Wales its fate is now linked with the curriculum 'free time' (which, as we have seen is likely to be very limited) and the success of the SOCRATES programme.

In Scotland the dimension has shown more tangible results: the teaching of foreign languages in the senior years of primary schools and a modest European component in the curriculum (see Scottish Consultative Council on the Curriculum, 1993.).

Many less specifically European collaborative initiatives can be derived from new attitudinal approaches in education. McLean's 'humanist tradition', most readily seen in the attention paid to individual educational development and the neglect of the role of the individual in society and the community, could be supplemented by the introduction of collaborative curriculum materials such as those outlined here and in Chapter 10. We see these initiatives flourishing when they are practised by pupils from schools in different countries addressing themselves to a topic in a collaborative fashion. Various 'activity' programmes, of personal concern to the pupils proceed to assume the form of large-scale European exchanges.

It is obvious that such initiatives might well form part of a programme of global education, extending beyond the relatively narrow boundaries of the European union, providing what would be a wider conception of 'European education'. Here the Council of Europe in Strasbourg shows itself perhaps more aware of new possibilities than the European Commission in Brussels does, which is much more constrained by European legislation and the rival concerns of individual member states.

The Implications of European Initiatives

The English neglect of education in terms of economic awareness to which Barnett (1986) has repeatedly drawn attention, is now being remedied, encouraged by the economic priorities of the European union. Even so, the development of work-experience schemes, which stimulated the Technical, Vocational and Economic Initiative (TVEI), did not easily integrate into the school curriculum. The General New Vocational Qualifications (GNVQ) schemes in England and Wales would seem to be bringing Britain closer to continental European practice where the two traditions of general and vocational education are to be found together. Following the Dearing Report of 1993 Britain is giving equal status to vocational and general education qualifications obtained at the end of compulsory schooling, at 16, a development similar to the case of the near parity of esteem bestowed by the different French *Baccalauréat* options.

The danger to this promising development may be the encouragement of schemes enabling English and Welsh schools to 'opt out' of local-authority control and devise their own patterns for the admission of pupils. England may be the first European country, with the exception of the tripartite system in parts of Germany, to be moving away from a largely comprehensive system of education and common curriculum before the end of compulsory schooling at 15 or 16 to one that will end up dividing pupils into 'academic' and 'vocational' routes at the early age of 14.

In recent years there have been school-curriculum innovations in a number of European-union countries which have allowed for the introduction of a local element into the school programme. The French have the *programme de l'école* (Bourdoncle and Cros, 1989) which allows each school to devote a part of the timetable to purely local priorities, characteristic of its region. This strongly resembles what we have called in Chapter 8 the 'local' element in teacher education. We would strongly support its presence at the school level as well, taking up a specifically allocated proportion of the timetable. Although the Germans have introduced more specialization in their last two years of schooling (Mitter, 1989; Kron, 1994), they have also introduced protected independent 'home room' time for their teachers (Kron, 1989).

The Dearing Report recommendation that a percentage of timetabled time should be available for schools to develop their own programmes of study, freed from the constraints of the National Curriculum, may, in effect, bring England and Wales closer to the pattern in other European countries. Thus, despite the central control achieved through the National Curriculum, there is, at least, a limited possibility of finding space for introducing a more firmly defined European dimension.

Europe as Experience

This is not the place to give full details of the various curriculum activities which would qualify as part of the European experience; however, the kind of activity which would be desirable can be easily sketched. Europe as *experience*, which addresses all of a pupil's capacities must not be allowed to become identified with absorbing Europe as *knowledge* alone. While including problems that young people living in Europe are faced with in their everyday lives, attempts at answering some socio-political, cultural, economic, and, indeed, religious and values questions will have to be made. As Reginald de Schryver (1994), when talking of what constitutes Europe's identity, says after quoting a variety of European artistic and cultural achievements:

> To this we should add, because they originated in Europe, . . . capitalism, industrial revolution, liberalism, socialism, democracy, etc., and alas some very common negative pages of our history such as colonialism, fascism, and connected with all that, the two world wars. (Schryver, 1994)

One could add other events, glorious and less glorious to the discussion. Examining, exploring, learning, or overcoming them together is a good guarantee for ensuring a firmer future for Europe.

This chapter has been broadly concerned with teaching about Europe

in schools. It is the one curriculum element which has been actively proposed for use in the schools of member states. It is the most elusive of
curriculum dimensions and so far can probably only be found in extra
curricular, affective and mobile cooperative activity. As such, it figures as
a component alongside the more cognitive approaches found within the
established curriculum.

These extra activities have proliferated as visits and exchanges in all
the member states, albeit with strong traditions of regional preferences.
As exchanges are exercises in interaction, in doing things together, it is
important to defend this feature against attempts to substitute knowledge,
as in 'subject-based knowledge', for them. It is desirable that involvement
with Europe should lead to a re-examination of attitudes amongst the
young, which could provide a base on which to build some of the other
curriculum aspects discussed.

Furthering the European dimension in education remains a difficult
task if we consider the variety of ways in which it can be tried. The
vocational element, which has proved successful in pupil exchanges, could
prove a good start, often linked with the more educational proposals we
have made (Blackledge, 1982). This would entail working experiences
abroad so as to give pupils a chance of doing things together and cement-
ing friendly relations in the future. Structured work exchanges of senior
pupils from France and Germany in England, as pioneered in Essex, giving them the opportunity of working, or observing, in a bank or super-
market for a week have been particularly successful in developing a sense
of European citizenship with its rights and duties, a feeling of what it is
like to live and work like 'a European'.

Overloading the curriculum must be resisted, especially with the slim-
ming-down exercise attempted by Dearing still untried. At a meeting in
July 1994 officers of the UKCEE preferred to distance themselves from a
scenario which would impose another curriculum element into a seem-
ingly empty slot.

Chapter 10

Developing the European Teacher

Identifying European Teacher Preparation

The teacher-education model we propose starts with the existing situation in a member state of the European union, in our case the United Kingdom, since, following Article 126 in Chapter 3 of the Treaty on Union, the curriculum of compulsory schooling remains a national concern. Whilst we personally favour closer European integration in all aspects of socio-political organization, including education, the programme we outline could also be acceptable to those who subscribe only to the provisions of the Single European Act and its concept of the mobility of the workforce. It is within these limits that we attempt to formulate suggestions how we can effectively educate teachers for a Europe that is likely to develop in the years after the Treaty on Union. Such development must be the result of a debate involving all the parties concerned, not just the administrators and legislators. It must especially involve the participation of teachers, teacher educators and student teachers.

This chapter, therefore, places the teacher–pupil relationship at the centre of all educational processes and transactions, in accordance with Recommendation 69 of the 1975 UNESCO meeting of Ministers of Education on the changing role of the teacher. It is in the course of their involvement with pupils, and in collaboration with other agents operating in the same or related fields, that teachers can make a substantial contribution to the socio-economic, political and cultural development of their communities. This complex brief has not always been adequately recognized in the status and remuneration of teachers' work.

More than any other forms of education, higher education, because of its intimate concern with the wider reaches of the political, social, cultural, scientific, medical, economic and religious areas of human endeavour, which have rarely remained confined within the narrow boundaries of a single nation state, has traditionally been more truly European than the more basic manifestations of life and schooling, such as subsistence and simple literacy and numeracy. This has been seen in the frequent exchanges of scholars between institutions, particularly from the Middle Ages onwards, resulting in similarities between courses and projects investigated and accomplished, leading to the mutual recognition of qualifications in areas such as theology, medicine, and philosophy, little affected by exclusively national priorities.

Secular teacher education was never a fully integrated part of the higher-education tradition, unlike the Europe-wide international collaboration in the training of clerics, at least until the Reformation, and to a lesser extent afterwards. In recent times, the European tradition in academic life has been significantly enlarged by the growing number of non-European scholars coming to European institutions to seek the prestige provided by long established institutions, which itself carries on a much older tradition not necessarily confined to Europe. What we are witnessing in a modern form is the spread of the tradition of the 'wandering scholar'; what we would like to see is a significant extension of the mobility and access between European cultural and academic institutions already available, especially in the education of teachers in member states of the European union. Similar, if not identical, ideas have been disseminated by the Council of Europe in Strasbourg (EAT and ERGTSE, 1993).

In making our proposals we are aware that the national structure of systems of teacher education often means that teachers are trained to work in a particular locality, or a particular type of school, with the result that their intellectual and socio-political horizons and their expectations are somewhat limited. Since, in the New Europe, they may eventually have to teach in very different circumstances and surroundings from those in which they were originally trained, the Treaty on Union has recognized the need for collaboration and exchange of information. The institutionalization of professional and vocational mobility by the Single European Act, has advanced the desirability of at least some broad common features in training and, indeed, education, if teachers' professional opportunities in all member states of the European Union are to be improved and to resemble more those of other professions and trades. Regrettably, not much rapid progress has been made to date.

Our concept of teacher education in Europe in the twenty-first century consists of three components:

1 **personal education** for which a broadly based curriculum from 16 to 19, such as the International Baccalaureate provides, is an essential preparation;
2 **professional education**; and
3 **European education**, which, through schemes such as SOCRATES, might also impinge upon personal education.

All teachers should experience this 'Europeanized' teacher preparation, the details of which are not incompatible with the general scheme of teacher preparation sketched earlier in Chapter 1 and which fit the scheme of teacher education given in the Introduction.

Following a general course of personal and academic education at both school and higher education, it is generally accepted that the starting point for intending teachers must be subject-knowledge, that is their academic discipline. Indeed it has been contended by some that subject knowledge, such as school mathematics, is all that an intending teacher needs, a reductionist view which disregards the need for the teacher to have a sound personal education as well as a professional preparation.

Consecutive preparation models, such as in England and Wales the Postgraduate Certificate of Education (PGCE) differentiate between subject knowledge and professional education: degree courses are not designed primarily as a preparation for teaching. In all subject areas there is a need, therefore, for those undergoing PGCE courses to have new and additional areas of knowledge developed which have not always been covered in their degree courses. These might include, for example, that of language awareness, also known as 'knowledge about language', for those teaching the mother tongue and the oral skills in modern foreign languages. Botany does not always feature as part of a course in biology. Because all school subjects now have to be taught in the context of the multicultural societies increasingly to be found in Europe, subject knowledge and skills need to be supplemented by additional areas dealing with concerns such as the European dimension, citizenship and intercultural education, and the care of the environment.

Undue insistence upon the subject discipline alone may deliver a pattern for teaching which is solely one of knowledge transmission controlled by national priorities. The very structures of degree courses are, in most cases, concerned with the acquisition of cognitively based knowledge and there is little attention paid, except in some fine arts subjects and drama, where taught, to the affective and psychosomatic domains of education and to the processes involved in knowledge acquisition, an element which is particularly lacking in the teaching of modern foreign languages. The degree course often educates to a tradition which, certainly to begin with, may be bewilderingly different from that to which the pupil is ready to respond. The European context, with its ideals and challenges, further compounds the difficulties experienced by many pupils, which teachers, educated within a narrow range of experience and specialist knowledge, are but inadequately prepared to meet.

Pupils' problems were recognized in England and Wales as long ago as the Crowther Report of 1959 which was already drawing attention to the large number of young people staying on at school beyond the official leaving age for whom a traditional academic 'sixth-form' education was in no way suitable. With the move away from the grammar-school-based 'tripartite' system, new structures for the post-16 curriculum were needed. Crowther instituted a debate which has been going on for more than thirty years and, given the survival power of the traditional Advanced Level examination or of the German *Abitur*, seems likely to go on for a considerable time to come.

In 1966, there was a joint agreement by the Schools Council for Curriculum and Examinations and the Standing Conference on University Entrance (SCUE) that three broad principles should inform curriculum reform for the 16–19 age range. These were that:

- the prospective increase in the size and academic range of sixth-form populations makes curriculum reform necessary to meet the various needs of sixth-formers;
- it is desirable to reduce specialization and broaden the scope of study in the sixth form;
- it is desirable that a pupil's choice of subjects for study in the sixth form and the university, insofar as it narrows career opportunities, should be made as late as possible.

These principles are worth recalling today. They are even more important in the light of the population explosion, the socio-political diversity of populations, the variety of job opportunities, and the challenge of the fresh responsibilities of the 'New Europe'. These call for a rethink of the curriculum, of changes in the structures of educational provision, and of new styles of teaching.

The three elements proposed in this chapter, which are not to be taken separately but which interrelate, aim to widen the horizons sketched in, not just nationally, but internationally.

1 Personal education

Personal education for prospective teachers must include development as persons through intellectual development in a subject, not necessarily, though frequently, the one to be taught in school. After all, as we have argued, university discipline areas only rarely coincide with school subject areas. Personal education must be widened through a series of collective experiences, such as those provided by producing a play, playing in a concert, or being responsible for organizing a joint project. Such activities, though of great value for personal development, are, in traditional higher-education courses, generally relegated to the position of optional or leisure activities. We would wish more status and greater importance accorded to them.

2 Professional education

Professional education will mean the recognition that there is such a subject as school mathematics and explore the different ways of teaching it, together with the classroom skills specific to the context of the mathematics classroom. The same applies equally in all areas of the school curriculum. The classroom skills required in a science laboratory or in a modern-languages classroom will differ from each other although there will also be some generalizable principles of classroom management, which the teacher must possess, underlying the teaching of all subjects. Even here, however, there will be considerable differences created by the ages and abilities of the pupils taught. There is, therefore, a considerable continuing role for the education of the prospective teacher in what we have called 'methods and curriculum studies', which should, as we have indicated in our mathematics example, include the principles underlying the content of the school treatment of the subject concerned, which will view mathematics across the curriculum in more than one school. Such studies are an inescapable part of the preparation of all teachers of pupils for the compulsory and post-compulsory years of schooling and necessary, therefore, for both primary and secondary teachers. In addition, what we have identified above as a part of personal education in the affective or psycho-somatic domains, may also form part of professional preparation.

3 European education

A teacher who is to be mobile in the New Europe will need to be aware that the skills required, both specific and general, may not necessarily be the same in different countries as a consequence of differences in social customs and attitudes. The development of empathy in this respect, a sensitivity towards, and respect for, the institutions and the feelings of others, is another important part of the professional preparation of the teacher.

The European context will include such areas as knowledge of the educational systems of Europe; teaching in multicultural classrooms and the development of an intercultural curriculum (see King and Reiss, 1993); developing awareness of other people's languages in their socio-political contexts which is not the same as complementing their language skills (Tulasiewicz, 1994), the function of European citizenship and the role of Europe within the wider world. European education will also include its own element of affective education through a concern with such areas as European architecture, art, music and literature. These are some of the items which are included within the European dimension in the 1993 Green Paper on *The European Dimension of Education* (op.cit.) and in pamphlets produced by the Council of Europe, such as the one entitled, *Teaching about Society, Passing on Values — Elementary Law and Civic Education*. European education should, however, also include other affective elements in the education of the teacher, such as that of the understanding and sensitivity to others, which, surprisingly, do not figure in the Green Paper or in other definitions of the European dimension. Education for Mutual Understanding (EMU), however, has already been identified as a curriculum ingredient in some Northern Ireland teacher-preparation courses (Farren, 1994).

We have written extensively about European education not only because we wish to emphasize it as a specific area, but because we are convinced that the best personal and professional education of future teachers in Europe will be enhanced by the inclusion of such a programme.

The Content of European Education

In modules for European education five elements will co-exist. These may be defined as follows:

- **Contents**: the cognitive element, the factual knowledge to be transmitted to the learner and evaluated by the ability to recall;
- **Concepts**: what the learner can intellectually generalize from the content and use to delimit it from other content areas and concepts, evaluated by the ability to explain;
- **Skills**: the procedures by which the learner is able to make the learning process both effective and efficient and evaluated by the ability to apply it in real or simulated situations;
- **Attitudes**: the affect that the learner brings to the learning activity and the values that are developed as a consequence of the learning, evaluated by observable change in behaviour;
- **Experiences**: the totality of all that has made up the learning experience so far and which has been integrated into the *persona* of the learner demonstrated by a willingness to participate.

Such a model for curriculum development has been used before in the preparation of teachers of the humanities (Adams, 1976) but we suggest that it is especially illuminating in the case of European education. For example, in a learning activity such as 'travel', already often used in school and class exchanges and visits in Europe and likely to be developed further under the SOCRATES and LEONARDO proposals, we might have the following paradigm:

- **Contents**: What would the place to be visited be like? This is the purely 'guide book' understanding of 'place', still to be found in school tours.
- **Concepts**: How does the place to be visited relate to other places with which I am familiar? This is to enable the new experience to be integrated with existing knowledge and experience, and to develop new concepts such as a European dimension.
- **Skills**: How do I manage to get to the place I wish to visit? This is to enable the skills of travelling, for example the efficient reading of airline or train timetables, map-reading skills, booking of accommodation and the like, together with the necessary associated language skills to make communication possible in a new environment. This also emphasizes possible vocational skills to be developed to improve pupils' chances of employment.
- **Attitudes**: How do I relate to the new environment, people, food, buildings, when I am there? This is to invoke the affective elements of the educational process which we have discussed earlier,

helping the more reluctant Europeans to feel comfortable in Europe.

- **Experiences**: What happens to me when I am there and what happened to me on my journey? This is an involvement of the psycho-motor and somatic elements of the curriculum inseparable from the already established cognitive and affective ones. It represents the *totality* of the learning experience, essential if full advantage is to be taken of all the provisions of the Single European Act of 1986.

The gloss under each heading tends to get longer as we move from the first to the last. This is because in many ways they constitute a hierarchy: content, generally accorded primacy in much conventional education, is, in a way, least important; most pupils do have a repertoire of a 'rag-bag' of facts at their disposal but do not know what to do with them. Attitudes and experiences are more important by far in educating school pupils, students and student teachers, who see themselves as 'European'. The goals also become more personalized as the hierarchy develops. The teacher, the 'pilot', is gradually jettisoned, or at least plays a less important role, as the learning experience is integrated into the personality of the learners who increasingly take over more responsibility for their own learning.

We suggest that as a further paradigm this could be developed in the following exemplars which should be included within a total European curriculum experience:

- tourism;
- language awareness;
- environmental monitoring;
- information technology;
- media studies; and
- citizenship.

some of which can be found explicitly mentioned in the SOCRATES and LEONARDO programmes, or found in the Council of Europe publications, such as *Teaching for Exchanges* (EAT and ERGTSE, op.cit.)

Significant portions of these are already being taught as cross-curricular elements in the programmes of some educational institutions. Indeed, each may be linked with conventional curriculum programmes already in existence in national educational systems, for example, 'tourism' may be linked with 'geography', and 'language awareness' with 'mother tongue' or 'modern foreign languages' education. At the same time they also have the potential of being developed into a European experience. Some of them, for example 'information technology' and 'media studies' can be seen both as a means of delivery of other aspects of the curriculum as well as being curriculum areas worthy of study in their own right.

This may be seen in the use of information technology to activate a programme in teacher education dealing with the European dimension and the world of work (Convey, 1992). Working in Leeds with a group of PGCE students being prepared to teach French, Françoise Convey devised a project whereby school pupils were to:

take part in 'simulated work experience in an adult working environment' . . . it stressed . . . two essential elements of language teaching, (a) the use of authentic materials and documents, and (b) the development of learner autonomy' . . .

The focal points . . . for the students were:
1 The re-use of known materials in a professional context; e.g. the writing of a letter or the use of the telephone.
2 The practicality of the work undertaken, its relevance to the needs of future employment . . .
3 The acquisition of skills in the use of a variety of means of communication and new technology . . . Real advances are taking place all the time and new computing equipment, satellite television and data-bases such as Minitel are becoming more commonplace . . . It was felt . . . particularly important for the team to face up to unfamiliar technologies . . .
4 The undertaking of genuine tasks involving several EC languages, e.g. writing a letter or using the telephone in the appropriate language in response to various advertisements . . . executed in various Community languages . . .
5 The comparison of pupils' attitudes towards different Community languages; this complemented the original survey conducted by the students . . . on the perception of Europe amongst pupils.
6 The crucial role of the enjoyment of the experience perceived as 'fun' and the appreciation of the opportunity to . . . develop contacts with peers in other European countries . . .

A selection of activities which [the school] pupils might expect to encounter while on work experience would include:
• Job advertisements;
• Application for a job;
• Writing a CV;
• Interview;
• Use of Minitel as a data-base or source of information;
• Use of telephone for booking a hotel or hiring a car; and
• Writing a telex or sending a fax. (Convey, 1992)

It will be readily seen that such a project exemplifies the five principles of curriculum design outlined above and that it is set firmly within the socio-economic context of vocational preparation in a single Europe. It also achieves an integration of some of the elements of 'tourism', 'information technology', 'media studies', 'language awareness' and 'citizenship' to which we have also alluded. Françoise Convey's project was part of an initial teacher-education course.

In the University of Cambridge, Kenneth Turner has developed an International 'Environmental Monitoring' project, which is primarily aimed at an in-service level. This drew upon the work of the Association for Science Education of the United Kingdom which, as reported by Turner in an internal paper prepared for the European Education Regional Partnership based in Hertfordshire:

> with support from British Petroleum, launched the *Science across Europe* programme [publishing] curriculum materials in nine European languages on a number of topics which occur commonly in national science and environmental curricula . . . By establishing collaboration between teachers and their 15 to 17 plus year classes in schools from seven countries, students [were] enabled to study specific environmental problems . . . and relate their first-hand investigations to the general problems of managing the environment . . . By using the latest data logging apparatus, software and electronic mail . . . the opportunity [existed] to develop . . . advanced techniques for the capture and exchange of environmental data in collaborative studies on the environment. The students will:
> * bring a basis in the traditional curriculum subject areas [to contribute] important background knowledge on environmental issues;
> * readily recognize the inherent conflicts of interest in most environmental issues;
> * be . . . capable of mounting investigations which they sustain without over-close supervision;
> * [be] able to sustain team work;
> * be expected to communicate successfully with outside agencies, write valid reports . . . and present their findings to the general public; and
> * use the latest electronic communication techniques.

Teacher training is integral to the design of the project since International projects and successful environmental education both require teachers often to develop expertise in a radically different form of pedagogy to their traditional subject-orientated teaching, as well as handling new technologies for international communication.

In this project several elements from what has been discussed above: environmental monitoring and information technology, as well as the undertaking of tasks involving several EC languages, are to be found, with pupils from different countries collaborating and teachers continuing to develop similar projects.

A third example falls into the area we have called language awareness. By this we understand 'language and its study based upon the latest linguistic principles in mother tongue languages and modern foreign language teaching' (as stated by the authors in 1993 in a submission to Brussels commenting on the Green Paper on *The European Dimension in Education*). While teaching language skills as a tool of effective communication, the cultural and social (as well as linguistic) aspects of language are introduced alongside the usual more specifically grammatical and stylistic elements.

This definition of critical language awareness envisages the use of language across three dimensions: instrumental, affective, and emancipatory. These three aspects should be made explicit to teachers and pupils throughout Europe to enable them to recognize language as a powerful instrument for good or ill. If we accept that language expresses identity, enables cooperation and confers freedom, we need in a European (and indeed worldwide) context to find ways of reconciling the identity expressed by one's own language with that experienced by others in their languages. That aspect of language awareness concerned with linguistic sensitivity encourages tolerance and respect for the rights and dignity of all cultural groups and alerts users to be open to other cultures. It is these cultures that contribute to the development of the New Europe. The writers have piloted courses in language awareness and knowledge about language in schools and HEIs of several countries. (Tulasiewicz, 1993b)

Language awareness enables one to see how language is acquired, how it works and how one uses language to achieve communication. The case for projects in language awareness as a basis for developing Europe-wide programmes of education is inescapable. Issues such as citizenship and ecology might well be discussed in Flemish or French in Belgium or in English in England, but cross-cultural discussion needs the development of a common 'language' to enable it to take place. In the threefold approach to language study suggested: involving areas of skills, awareness and sensitivity, and tolerance, the language base of future young Europeans is being developed.

Non-British Initiatives

In presenting these three British examples we do not wish to minimalize the contribution to work along similar lines to be found elsewhere in Europe. Initiatives such as the European clubs in Portuguese schools, referred to earlier in the book, together with the border-area study exchanges mentioned later, as well as the European-studies project based at the Ulster Folk and Transport Museum, supported by education authorities in France, Belgium, the *Land* of Berlin, and the Lothian Regional Council in Scotland (Convey, 1992) must be mentioned. The general support available for European proposals from the Central Bureau for Educational Visits and Exchanges and the United Kingdom Centre for European Education (see Chapter 8) qualifies as a European initiative.

Other encouraging European initiatives have been underway for some years, like the requirement of a modern foreign language for all teachers in training at the Roehampton Institute, and the cross-border cooperations between HEIs in the Rhineland-Palatinate and Alsace, in Frankfurt (Oder) and Słubice, and in Białystok and Grodno, which lead to the award of European and joint local diplomas after extended periods of study amongst foreign neighbours.

The exemplars we have given show that European education does not consist of the acquisition of cognitive information alone but needs to be supported by direct European experience, either of travelling or working abroad, or through involvement in curriculum-based projects using information technology as a means of communication and investigation. The latter is especially useful when helping pupils from several countries to focus on particular aspects of their school curriculum. We would argue that, given the necessary financial support, more likely to be forthcoming with the new SOCRATES and LEONARDO proposals, all teachers in training should spend some of their school practice experience in another European country than their own (Kodron, 1993).

The choice of examples is also intended to draw attention to the importance of seeing teacher education as a continuum embracing initial teacher education, a process of induction (the probationary period), and continuing (in-service) education for teachers, which is not all that frequent. For example the German teacher-training programmes effectively split education from professional preparation. These cannot really be separated from each other since, as we have shown earlier in Chapter 4, the same person can be, at the same time, trainee, mentor and tutor at any stage of their professional development.

The pattern of a three-stage process of teachers' professional development is, in fact, to be found in all the other European member states discussed in this book and was only recently curtailed in England and Wales with the abolition of the probationary year of service. In our suggested scheme in-service education, as proposed in SOCRATES, is suited to developing the European dimension, though we feel that there is a place for this in initial teacher education also. Many of the ingredients of our suggestions are already in place which, given the will, should make the systematic introduction of a specifically European education for teachers relatively easy.

European Education Proposals and the Maastricht Exclusion Zones

Despite the sterling work done by organized networks such as the RIF, discussed in Chapter 8, the supremacy of national sovereignty in matters of education, has made it possible in the field of teacher education for member states of the European union to be reluctant to agree on common programmes of study across Europe, of which a prime example is the failure to emphasize the European dimension as a fundamental component. This is in contrast to the vocational programmes, such as PETRA, which regard the 'uneven development of training resources in the different regions of the Community' as serious negative factors 'affecting the economic and social cohesion of the Community' (Welbers, 1993). It is interesting that these views were expressed (June 1993) many months after the Treaty on Union with its reservations about harmonization in education had been approved. Welbers emphasizes that practical European experience has a strong effect on young people's awareness of the European union and goes on to plead for the 'added value' of more union-supported approaches to training and the introduction of a European dimension into existing vocational preparation courses.

The significance of the PETRA priorities for the suggestions put forward in this chapter is that they specifically acknowledge the economic advantages to be gained alongside the more general raising of standards and the quality of initial vocational training patterns, the potential of which has not as yet been fully realized in teacher education (PETRA, 1993). In fact, the PETRA vocational proposals demonstrate a better sense of adaptation to economic, social and technological change than do teacher education programmes, by encouraging young people themselves to take the initiative in devising their own 'mobile' programmes of study.

All this is in marked contrast to the requirements of the National Curriculum in England and Wales and the arrangements made for its assessment where, for example, despite the opposition of the teaching profession, the quantity of coursework, which may be submitted by pupils, so allowing for diversity, has been dramatically reduced. As was made clear in the Government's statements subsequent to the publication of the National Curriculum Council's report on primary education (Alexander, Rose and Woodhead, 1992), those in positions of power are determined to impose teacher-led procedures on the schools.

The 'Value-added' Contribution of the European Teacher

European teachers we have encountered in shared-experience projects would not be satisfied simply to pass on subject knowledge to their pupils but would wish to contribute to actively shaping the society in which they work. They would moreover see it as part of their duty to share their own awareness with their pupils. The multifaceted character of education referred to in the Introduction requires adaptable teachers with vision, those who can justly be regarded as members of a major profession. Much *physical* mobility has been facilitated and encouraged by existing European programmes; however, mobility has also to be an *intellectual* mobility, with all the flexibility and tolerance that this entails.

To achieve this, it is essential that European teachers are given the fullest support during their training to become aware of what the European dimension precisely stands for, expressed in terms of their pupils' concrete needs in Europe: not merely the language and social skills, but the opportunity to reflect on their own attitudes and priorities, a point made by Roland Vandenberghe, speaking at a symposium organized by the RIF at Leuven in 1993. An 'open state of mind' is what characterizes the European teacher, someone who, in a regional group, is willing to discuss and work together with others in an approach 'without parochialism, in a national one, without chauvinism, and a universal one, without Europhobia', to paraphrase Reginald de Schryver speaking on the same occasion.

We have stressed throughout the need for a European *experience* in preference to a purely cognitive diet of facts and concepts. In this respect we endorse the view of the Canadians, Clandinin and Connelly, on the importance of a 'knowledge which is experiential, embodied and reconstructed out of the narrative of a teacher's life' (Clandinin and Connelly, 1987). We would add that this is exactly the sense in which the pupil too has to be educated. Our earlier paradigms put experience at the apex of a pupil's activities, an experience which is not to be confined to a national, in our case a uniquely British one. We are convinced that it is possible to introduce a European experience, which includes all the factors listed, even within the constraints imposed on education allowed for by the Treaty.

The important thing about the Treaty with its provision of a legal basis for fuller cooperation between member states of the European union is that the route is clear for a joint effort to address the educational challenges which teachers are facing and which they will continue to face in the twenty-first century in attending to the needs of their pupils in the European context.

Concluding Remarks

The actual teacher-preparation components of the European teacher are those which have been identified earlier in this book. After a period of personal study, which may increasingly contain various European modules, the new practitioners proceed to their professional training, to be completed in both HEIs and schools. This phase of teacher preparation, too, should include European elements, involving a significant part of the practical training to be spent in another country.

For the smooth running of collaborative schemes some degree of harmonization is inevitable. However, it must be repeated that in this respect current English education practice is running against trends and developments in the other member states of the European union, the most blatant of which is the call for a return to 'basics', a deliberate search for the past rather than a look forward to future challenges, an insular stance not shared with other European-union countries, underlined by the virtual elimination of higher education in the *professional* preparation part of teacher education in the ways that we have described, impeding the emergence of a successful collaboration with our partners in Europe and elsewhere.

We regret that more opportunity has not been taken by critics of teacher education, as it now exists, to mention the failure to include provision for a European dimension with periods of training spent abroad, while acknowledging the constructive general involvement of the National Association of Teachers in Higher and Further Education (NATFHE) or the National Associations of Head Teachers, especially through its European agency the European Secondary Heads Association (ESHA) with their comments on the British reforms, some of which we have quoted.

In both the existing and proposed programmes of teacher education in England and Wales, there is little opportunity to compare British practice in education with that in the rest of Europe to study the topic of education in European society. What particularly concerns us is that teacher preparation as education is often formulated by those who have had little to do with education as schooling, so that while their structures may reflect various pluralist or minimalist intervention policies they are not based on extensive studies of the schooling process itself. This goes for curriculum development, assessment policies which are affected by an outlook, a vision of society and formulated theory, which pays little attention to Europe, except insofar as some curriculum measures, such as the teaching of modern foreign languages, might be regarded as more competitively desirable in economic terms.

There is little doubt that, within the provisions of the Single European Act, let alone the Treaty on Union, teachers will have to be trained for their role in international collaborative projects. International projects and the particular educational topics they will be more and more assisting with will require teachers to develop expertise in a radically different form of pedagogy to their traditional subject-orientated teaching. They will have to begin cooperation with agencies such as adult education, distance learning, parents' associations, and particularly with international projects involving educational innovation, such as telematics, or European union-assisted projects, such as TEMPUS. Constant updating in these areas will require a concerted effort to increase in-service preparation, which can best be done by pooling resources in association with European partners.

We are pleased to conclude that the 100 per cent school-based teacher-training scheme at Bromley, which we have referred to elsewhere, has indeed recognized the importance of a European element in its preparation of teachers, all of whom will spend a week in France as part of the scheme. This may not be unrelated to the existence of the Channel Tunnel and its location in nearby Folkestone.

Conclusion

Even a cursory examination of teacher-training practices reveals that for the most part they originate with responses to the immediate needs of schooling and continue in accordance with traditionally accepted structures and institutions on an incremental pattern. Change can hardly be said to be based on a sustained analysis of the professional needs of teachers, nor does it often assume vast dimensions. While we have argued that the first is true, the same can certainly not be said for the second in view of the scale of the revolutionary educational changes still proceeding in England and Wales. But professional preparation of teachers not only takes account of the teaching situation in schools; in turn it affects the schools, when they are used for the periods of practical experience.

Reform of educational provision, including teacher training, for the socio-political, economic, cultural, demographic and environmental conditions of the twenty-first century, as in the case of the compulsory training of secondary-school teachers, must continue to abolish anachronisms. It must be based not only on an assessment of present needs, but include a careful analysis of possible future developments. In view of the limits imposed by the lack of resources, both human and material, the expected outcome and cost of change must be calculated much more clearly than has been the case with the teacher-education reforms in England and Wales. Reform may well have to be sufficiently flexible to be capable of further change, if necessary, so as to adjust priorities recognized in subject content and professional theory and their application in practice. Debate involving all the participants, professional educators as well as educated politicians, should precede reform to ensure that the changes do not amount to *ad hoc* responses to divert funding or to satisfy narrowly ideological or national criteria.

It could be argued that improving school education ought to be a higher priority than large-scale reforms of teacher education so as to make schools, as institutions, more acceptable to the pupils. More lawbreaking than ever is being committed by people who are still of compulsory education age. In Germany this is the major point of current educational debate. The problem cannot be remedied by the simple expedient of raised intellectual standards. It is frightening that there are teachers who advocate the rote learning of facts of English history without bothering to suggest what pupils could actually *do* with this information. In an article in the

Daily Telegraph (5 May 1994) the writer complained 'that not a single British monarch was prescribed . . .' and went on to suggest that pupils should remember that 'knowledge about our country's history [is] their birthright'. A diet of such facts will hardly enable pupils to grasp the complex political, economic, technological and scientific, social, religious, cultural and aesthetic perspectives and problems which face them.

Though the aims of history teaching in Germany and Poland, where, unlike in England, the subject has to be taught until the school-leaving age and is linked with civic and political education, are perhaps not significantly less nationalistic, they do include attention to current developments and challenges in Europe and show how they have roots in the past. For young adolescents to be involved they must be taught curriculum items so as to help them to become engaged, a job every teacher should be prepared to assist with.

The ever-increasing interdependence of nations makes international consultation essential. However, although there has been collaboration in the areas of European and environmental education syllabuses in the European context, international cooperation in classroom practice or teacher preparation has not been identified as a priority.

In keeping with the economic and market priorities identified in Britain, education reform in England and Wales sees pupils' needs almost exclusively in terms of their entitlement to a curriculum useful to themselves, principally addressing the provision of compulsory subjects to be taught. It is necessary for education planners and curriculum developers to acknowledge the close link between lessons held in the classroom and on the playing fields, between work and leisure, here and abroad, and to work for interaction of all pupils and staff which is essential for both social harmony and efficient teaching.

Alternative models of teacher education must take over from those aiming for the overused rhetoric of 'quality'. Definitions of quality do not mention the principle of interdependence. This is so both at the macro level of international cooperation and at the micro level of individual student performance in terms of the individual as a member of a large group. Running projects involving the active participation of communities, be they communities of pupils or teachers in training, to do with environmental protection or communication, for example, does not as a rule figure in teacher-preparation courses though it has been identified in Poland. It would enable pupils to learn the art of cooperation and to grow up in an atmosphere where transnational concerns take first place. Topics such as citizenship, human rights or the environment are a challenging task for an education concerned with a united Europe.

Comparative study has a role to play in this. Unfortunately, what may be believed to be the adoption of a foreign model, is usually the introduction of a model chosen by the educational authorities of the nation state acting alone and in that nation's interests. Our concept of the European teacher recognizes the need to act together, a new criterion which to date, not only in Britain, has not been seriously considered in teacher education. Collaboration and consultation in education, the involvement of teachers and students, the importance of education proved by the spate of national legislation throughout Europe, are both a problem and a challenge for the European Union.

The present reforms proposed or underway in both the economic and political spheres in many countries make this the right time for professional, academic and public opinion, including business interests, such as identified in the Report of the National Commission on Education to proclaim their concern for education, to be heard besides those of government and seek solutions other than those based on a fashionable ideology.

Articles 126 and 127 of the Treaty on European Union (the Maastricht Treaty)

Article 126

1 The Community shall contribute to the development of quality education by encouraging co-operation between member states and, if necessary, by supporting and supplementing their action, while fully respecting the responsibility of the member states for the content of teaching and the organisation of education systems and their cultural and linguistic diversity.

2 Community action shall be aimed at:
   * developing the European dimension in education, particularly through the teaching and dissemination of the languages of the member states;
   * encouraging mobility of students and teachers, *inter alia* by encouraging the academic recognition of diplomas and periods of study;
   * promoting co-operation between educational establishments;
   * developing exchanges of information and experience on issues common to the education systems of the member states;
   * encouraging the development of youth exchanges and of exchanges of socio-educational instructors;
   * encouraging the development of distance education.

3 The Community and the member states shall foster co-operation with third countries and the competent international organisations in the field of education, in particular the Council of Europe.

4 In order to contribute to the achievement of the objectives referred to in this article, the Council:
   * acting in accordance with the procedure referred to in Article 189b, after consulting the Economic and Social Committee and the Committee of the Regions, shall adopt incentive measures, excluding any harmonisation of the laws and regulations of the member states;
   * acting by a qualified majority on a proposal from the Commission, shall adopt recommendations.

Article 127

1   The Community shall implement a vocational training policy which shall support and supplement the action of the member states, while fully respecting the responsibility of the member states for the content and organisation of vocational training.
2   Community action shall aim to:
- facilitate adaptation to industrial changes, in particular through vocational training and retraining;
- improve initial and continuing vocational training in order to facilitate vocational integration and re-integration into the labour market;
- facilitate access to vocational training and encourage mobility of instructors and trainees and particularly young people;
- stimulate co-operation on training between educational or training establishments and firms;
- develop exchanges of information and experience on issues common to the training systems of the member states.
3   The Community and the member states shall foster co-operation with third countries and the competent international organisations in the sphere of vocational training.
4   The Council, acting in accordance with the procedure referred to in Article 189c and after consulting with the Economic and Social Committee, shall adopt measures to contribute to the achievement of the objectives referred to in this Article, excluding any harmonisation of the laws and regulations of the member states.

It should be noted that the European union, under the terms of Article 126, will encourage development of the European dimension with the implications discussed in our Chapter 8. It will fully respect the cultural and linguistic diversity of the member states and their responsibility for the content of teaching and the organization of their educational systems. Article 126 is supported by Article 57 which gives the Council of Ministers the power to issue directives for the mutual recognition of diplomas, certificates and other evidence of formal qualifications.

The references to Articles 189 (b) and 189 (c) are important because in the field of education the Council of Ministers will adopt measures on a qualified majority vote, with the European Parliament having the right of amendment and veto. In the case of vocational training the Parliament has a right of amendment but not one of veto.

Further discussion of these issues can be found in *A Curriculum for Europe*, published by the Further Education Unit in London in 1994.

Competences Expected of Newly Qualified Teachers in England, Wales and Scotland

Reprinted here are the details of the competences expected of newly qualified teachers in England, Wales and Scotland. These come, in the case of England and Wales, from DFE Circular 9/92 (25 June) and the corresponding Welsh Office Circular 35/92 of the same date: 'Initial Teacher Training (Secondary Phase)', and, in the case of Scotland, from the Scottish Office Education Department's Guidelines for Teacher-training Courses, of August 1993.

The way the different competences have recently been formulated in the United Kingdom is less commonly found in other European countries where the teacher's competence in subject knowledge is the prime consideration.

The extracts are printed on facing pages to enable a comparison between the more professional concerns of the Scottish document influenced, as it undoubtedly is, by the GTC for Scotland. The English document, perhaps more like its European counterparts, tends to emphasize subject knowledge. The Scottish equivalent deals at greater length with classroom skills, distinguishing between school and wider professional concerns (such as communication with members of other professions concerned with children) and has a lengthy section on methodology. Its tone is much less authoritarian and prescriptive, giving it a more friendly and collegiate feel.

Appendix 2

Initial Teacher Training (Secondary Phase) Guidelines in England and Wales. DFE Circular 9/92 and Welsh Office Circular 35/92 — 25 June 1992.

2. *Competences Expected of Newly Qualified Teachers*

    2.1 Higher education institutions, schools and students should focus on the competences of teaching throughout the whole period of initial training. The progressive development of these competences should be monitored regularly during initial training. Their attainment at a level appropriate to newly qualified teachers should be the objective of every student taking a course of initial training.

Subject Knowledge

    2.2 Newly qualified teachers should be able to demonstrate:
      2.2.1 an understanding of the knowledge, concepts and skills of their specialist subjects and of the place of these subjects in the school curriculum;
      2.2.2 knowledge and understanding of the National Curriculum and attainment targets (NCATs) and the programmes of study (PoS) in the subjects they are preparing to teach, together with an understanding of the framework of the statutory requirements;
      2.2.3 a breadth and depth of subject knowledge extending beyond PoS and examination syllabuses in school.

Subject Application

    2.3 Newly qualified teachers should be able to:
      2.3.1 produce coherent lesson plans which take account of NCATs and of the school's curriculum policies;
      2.3.2 ensure continuity and progression within and between classes and in subjects;
      2.3.3 set appropriately demanding expectations for pupils;
      2.3.4 employ a range of teaching strategies appropriate to the age ability and attainment level of pupils;
      2.3.5 present subject content in clear language and in a stimulating manner;
      2.3.6 contribute to the development of pupils language and communication skills;
      2.3.7 demonstrate ability to select and use appropriate resources, including Information Technology.

Scottish Office Education Department's Guidelines for Teacher-training Courses — August 1993

2. *The Competences*

   2.1 *Competences Relating to Subject and Content of Teaching*
   The new teacher should be able to: —
   - demonstrate a knowledge of the subject or subjects forming the content of his or her teaching which meets and goes beyond the immediate demands of the school curriculum;
   - plan generally, and in particular prepare coherent teaching programmes which ensure continuity and progression, taking into account national, regional and school curriculum policies and plan lessons within these teaching programmes;
   - select appropriate resources for learning, for example from radio and television broadcasts;
   - present the content of what is taught in an appropriate fashion to pupils;
   - justify what is taught from knowledge and understanding of the learning process, curriculum issues, child development in general and the needs of his or her pupils in particular.

   2.2 *Competences Relating to the Classroom*
   2.2.1 *Communication*
   The new teacher should be able to: —
   - present what he or she is teaching in clear language and a stimulating manner;
   - question pupils effectively, respond and support their discussion and questioning.

   2.2.2 *Methodology*
   The new teacher should be able to: —
   - employ a range of teaching strategies appropriate to the subject or topic and, on the basis of careful assessment, to the pupils in his or her classes;
   - identify suitable occasions for teaching the class as a whole, in groups, in pairs or as individuals;
   - create contexts in which pupils can learn;
   - set expectations which make appropriate demands on pupils;
   - identify and respond appropriately to pupils with special educational needs or with learning difficulties;
   - take into account cultural differences among pupils;
   - encourage pupils to take initiatives in, and become responsible for, their own learning;
   - select and use in a considered way a wide variety of resources, including information technology;
   - evaluate and justify the methodology being used.

Appendix 2

Class Management

2.4 Newly qualified teachers should be able to:

    2.4.1 decide when teaching the whole class, groups, pairs, or individuals is appropriate for particular learning purposes;

    2.4.2 create and maintain a purposeful and orderly environment for the pupils;

    2.4.3 devise and use appropriate rewards and sanctions to maintain an effective learning environment;

    2.4.4 maintain pupils' interest and motivation.

Assessment and Recording of Pupils' Progress

2.5 Newly qualified teachers should be able to:

    2.5.1 identify the current level of attainment of individual pupils using NCATs, statements of attainment and end of key stage statements where applicable;

    2.5.2 judge how well each pupil performs against the standard expected of a pupil of that age;

    2.5.3 assess and record systematically the progress of individual pupils;

    2.5.4 use such assessment in their teaching;

    2.5.5 demonstrate that they understand the importance of reporting to pupils on their progress and of marking their work regularly against agreed criteria.

2.2.3 *Class Management*
       The new teacher should have a knowledge of the principles which
       lie behind the keeping of good discipline and should be able to: —
       • deploy a range of approaches to create and maintain a purpose-
         ful, orderly and safe environment for learning;
       • manage pupil behaviour by the use of appropriate rewards and
         sanctions and be aware when it is necessary to seek advice;
       • sustain the interest and motivation of the pupils.
2.2.4 *Assessment*
       The new teacher should: —
       • have an understanding of the principles of assessment and the
         different kinds of assessment which may be used;
       • be able to assess the quality of pupils' learning against national
         standards defined for that particular group of pupils;
       • be able to assess and record systematically the progress of indi-
         vidual pupils;
       • be able to provide regular feedback to pupils on their progress;
       • be able to use assessment to evaluate and improve teaching.

Appendix 2

Further Professional Development

2.6   Newly qualified teachers should have acquired in initial training the necessary foundation to develop:

    2.6.1   an understanding of the school as an institution and its place within the community;

    2.6.2   a working knowledge of their pastoral, contractual, legal and administrative responsibilities as teachers;

    2.6.3   an ability to develop effective working relationships with professional colleagues and parents, and to develop their communication skills;

    2.6.4   an awareness of individual differences, including social, psychological, developmental and cultural dimensions;

    2.6.5   the ability to recognise diversity of talent including that of gifted pupils;

    2.6.6   the ability to identify special educational needs or learning difficulties;

    2.6.7   a self-critical approach to diagnosing and evaluating pupils' learning, including a recognition of the effects on that learning of teachers' expectations;

    2.6.8   a readiness to promote the moral and spiritual well-being of pupils.

2.3 *Competences Relating to the School*
    The new teacher should:
    - have some knowledge of the system in which he or she is working and in particular of the organisation and management systems of schools, of school policies and development plans and where they relate to his or her teaching;
    - know how to discuss with parents a range of issues relevant to their children;
    - be informed about school boards;
    - know how to communicate with members of other professions concerned with the welfare of a school's pupils and with members of the community served by the school, as well as with colleagues within the school and its associated schools;
    - be aware of sources of help and expertise within the school and how they can be used;
    - be aware of cross-curricular aspects of school work and be able to make an input into these;
    - have interests and skills which can contribute to activities with pupils outside the formal curriculum.

2.4 *Competences Related to Professionalism*
    The new teacher should:
    - have a working knowledge of his or her pastoral, contractual, legal and administrative responsibilities;
    - be able to make a preliminary evaluation of his or her own professional progress.

    However, professionalism implies more than a mere series of competences. It also implies a set of attitudes which have particular power in that they are communicated to those being taught: —
    - a commitment to the job and to those affected by the job;
    - a commitment to self-monitoring and continuing professional development;
    - a commitment to collaborate with others to promote pupil achievement;
    - a commitment to promoting the moral and spiritual well-being of pupils;
    - a commitment to the community within and beyond the school and to promoting a responsible attitude towards the needs of the environment;
    - a commitment to views of fairness and equality of opportunity as expressed in multicultural and other non-discriminatory policies.

Remit Letter for the Teacher Training Agency

In a letter dated 5 October 1994 the Secretary of State spelt out in detail the duties of the TTA, established on 21 September 1994. The TTA will take over from the Council for the Accreditation of Teacher Education the responsibility for developing profiles of competences of newly qualified teachers, such as those listed above.

Unlike the rest of Europe (including Scotland) where such matters are the responsibility of Ministers, guided by professional opinion, the TTA is a quango, composed of eleven appointed members largely representing the schools and the 'new' universities and omitting altogether representation from the long established universities, some of which (like Cambridge) have been engaged in teacher education for over a hundred years.

The Agency will, from 1 April 1995, take over the functions of accreditation and registration of all newly qualified teachers. In particular, training institutions will be accredited by the Agency subject to their provision of courses which satisfy the Secretary of State's criteria. It will work closely with the Office for Standards in Education (OFSTED) in establishing a continuing inspection regime. If accreditation is withdrawn no courses run by the institutions concerned will lead to qualified teacher status.

The TTA combines, therefore, in one body the functions of funding, accrediting, information gathering and disseminating and the development of classroom research in respect of teacher training, all of which had previously been administered separately. This contradicts the avowed aim of providing diversity, claimed for it in the Secretary of State's letter. There seem great dangers in concentrating so much unparalleled power over the future direction of teacher education in one wholly unelected body. In particular the argument for diversity, as ensuring balance between denominational and other provision and between school-centred initial teacher training and other provision, does not accord with the emphasis earlier in the letter on securing 'the involvement of schools in all courses for the initial training of school teachers'.

The creation of the TTA effectively takes teacher training out of the mainstream of higher education. As has already been pointed out by most of the teachers' unions, its wide powers indicate the need for a General Teachers' Council for England and Wales although, in practice, the very existence of the TTA with its multiple brief and control makes this less likely to be achieved.

Réseau d'Institutions de Formation (RIF) — Network of Training Institutions

The RIF is part of the ERASMUS Programme which seems likely to continue in some form after the incorporation of ERASMUS into SOCRATES. In September 1993 an important symposium was held in Leuven and Liège at which the various initiatives undertaken by the RIF subnetworks were described. This appendix lists the various subnetworks and their concerns at that time since they represent some of the most distinctive innovations in teacher education so far developed in the European union.

They are as follows:

Subnetwork 1: European Citizenship

France: Coordinated by the Institut universitaire de formation des maîtres (IUFM) de Paris, Centre des Batignolles, 56 Boulevard des Batignolles, 75017, Paris (Tel: 33-1-43.87.61.15/Fax: 33-1.-44.70.07.89).

This subnetwork is concerned to monitor the intensive mobility programme of teachers and students with the objective of proposing new structures to stimulate mobility. A general report has been published summarizing all the information so far collected.

Subnetwork 2: European Dimension, Human Rights and Values

Portugal: Coordinated by Escola Superior de Educaçao do Instituto Politecnico do Porto, R. Dr. Roberto Frias, 4200 Porto (Tel: 351-2-49. 11.40/Fax: 351-2-48.07.72).

This subnetwork is reflecting on concepts in relation to values and human rights through the European dimension in education which will result in the production of teaching materials, a picture book and training modules.

Subnetwork 3: The Training of School Directors to the European Dimension

United Kingdom: Coordinated by Jordanhill College, Southbrae Drive, Glasgow G13 1PP (Tel: 44-41-950.33.61/Fax: 44-41-950.32.68).

The key aim of this subnetwork is the training of headteachers for the European dimension. So far it has produced one publication, *Managing the European dimension in Schools* (B.T. Peck, Jordanhill College of Education, 1992). A further proposed publication is a training programme which the different countries of Europe can use for the in-service training of their headteachers in managing the changes they wish to introduce in their schools to integrate the European dimension.

Subnetwork 4: A Comparison of Educational and Training Systems

Belgium: Coordinated by the Association for Teacher Education in Europe, Rue de la Concorde, 60, 1050 Bruxelles (Tel: 32-2-514. 51. 81/Fax: 32-2-514.11.72) and Pedagogische Dienst NVKHO, Saint Adresse plein 12, 1070, Anderlecht (Tel: 32-2-529.04.29/Fax: 32-2-529.04.93).

This subnetwork is finalizing a reader on the introduction of the European dimension in teacher education for primary and secondary schools and the production of a series of videos showing how students are trying to introduce the European dimension in their training. It is also concerned with the construction of a parallel network with eastern Europe.

Subnetwork 5: The European Dimension and Primary Education

Ireland: Coordinated by Mary Immaculate College, South Circular Road, Limerick (Tel: 353-61-31.45.88/Fax: 353-61-31.36.32).

The activities of this subnetwork have resulted in a mobility programme, MEITHEAL, aiming at preparing student teachers for developing and delivering a basic curriculum on the European dimension in primary schools.

Subnetwork 6: The European Dimension and Secondary Education

Spain: Coordinated by Collegi de Doctors i Llicenciats en Filosofia, i Lletres i Ciencies de Catalunya, Rambla de Catalunya, 8 principal, 08007, Barcelona (Tel: 34-3-317.04.28/Fax 34-3-412.49.07) and Universitat de

Barcelona, Facultat de Pedagogia, c/ Baldiri I Reixac, s.n. 08028, Barcelona (Tel: 34-3-333.34.66 ext 3367/Fax: 34-3-334.91.93).

This subnetwork has been preparing a basic curriculum on the European dimension for use both in the training of secondary-school teachers and for those already in post in the secondary sector. It has also set up a mobility scheme for trainee teachers and those involved in in-service training by organizing a one-month module on introducing the European dimension into secondary-school teaching within the framework of an intensive ERASMUS programme.

Subnetwork 7: The European Dimension: The Development and Sharing of Materials in the Social Sciences

Belgium: Coordinated by Institut Supérieur Pédagogique Libre, Hors Chateau 61, 4000, Liège (Tel: 32-41-22.09.91/Fax: 32-41-21.14.29).

This subnetwork is preparing an experimental 'guide-book' on the introduction of the European dimension into social sciences in teacher education. A training module will be built on the pedagogical documents taken from the guide-book and a framework to analyze the landscapes hit by industrialization will be developed.

Subnetwork 8: The European Dimension: The Development and Sharing of Teaching Materials in the Scientific Disciplines

Portugal: Coordinated by Universidade de Lisboa, R. Ernesto Vasconcelos — Cl, 1700, Lisboa (Tel: 351-1-757.36.24/Fax: 351-1-757.36.24).

This subnetwork has published: *Teaching and learning sciences from 4–15: six case studies in Europe*. It is involved in mobility through ERASMUS and aims to support the work done to develop a new curriculum for science education based on modules.

Subnetwork 9: The Learning of Foreign Languages for a Better European Dimension in Education

The Netherlands: Coordinated by Hogeschool Gelderland, Centre for International Education, Postbus 30011, 6503 HN Nijmegen (Tel: 31-80-45.98.02/Fax: 31-80-44.97.94).

The main objective of this subnetwork is to raise the awareness that teaching a foreign language is teaching a foreign culture. It has reflected on the teaching of languages as a cultural vehicle and on the role of a language, or of certain languages, to be used as a *lingua franca*. It is working on a publication stressing the theoretical basis of its work and on a collection of examples of cross-cultural communication that can be used either as teaching materials or as examples of real-life communication to serve as sources of inspiration for the authors of textbooks.

Subnetwork 10: The European Dimension and the New Information Technologies

United Kingdom: Coordinated by Nottingham Trent University, Centre for In-Service Education, Clifton Lane, Nottingham NG11 8NS (Tel: 44-602-41.84.18 (ext 3425)/Fax: 44-602-48.66.26) and Nottingham Trent University, Department of Secondary and Tertiary Education, Burton Street, Nottingham NG1 4UB (Tel: 44-602-41.84.18 (ext. 2198)/Fax: 44-602-48.64.97).

This subnetwork has worked for two years preparing student mobility through an intensive ERASMUS programme for which it has developed ten modules focusing on ten themes related to new technologies and the European dimension. The final objective was to help the students prepare a module for the curriculum of pupils aged 4–14 using new technologies. A series of products have been produced by subgroups of students.

Subnetwork 11: The European Dimension and Cultural Patrimony

Greece: Coordinated by the University of Crete, Departement de Pedagogie, 74100, Rethymno (Tel: 30-831-280/Fax: 30-831-240.67).

The objective of this subnetwork has been to awaken a European consciousness starting from a common past so as to prepare a common future and stimulate student mobility. To reach them the group decided to work around one common theme from Greek mythology, 'the labyrinth'. A wide range of products in a variety of media are being prepared.

Subnetwork 12: The European Dimension in Environmental Education

Denmark: Coordinated by Odense Seminarium, Middelfartvej 180, 5200 Odense V (Tel: 45-66-16.94.32/Fax: 45-66-16.85.32).

The objective has been to increase awareness of teachers in training for environment by stimulating mobility. Two student mobility programmes have been organized through ERASMUS in which the students were invited to create common materials and tools which could be used in the classrooms of different European countries. The subnetwork will publish a manual based on its experiences.

Subnetwork 13: The European Dimension and Multiculturalism

Germany: Coordinated by Pädagogische Hochschule Freiburg, Kunzenweg 21, 79117, Freiburg (Tel: 49-761-68.23.19/Fax: 49-761-68.24.02).

The subnetwork has reflected on the concepts of multiculturalism and interculturalism in relation to the European dimension. It has organized, through ERASMUS, student-mobility programmes on 'Intercultural education and the European dimension in a multicultural Europe', in which the students jointly developed tools and materials for teaching. It is preparing a documentation file in different languages for teacher trainers and students not yet involved in the RIF which will include draft guidelines for the evaluation of projects in the field of intercultural education and the European dimension.

Subnetwork 14: The European Dimension and Disabled Children, or Children having Difficulties at School

Italy: Coordinated by IRRSAE Lombardia, Istituto Regionale di Ricerca, Sperimentazonie e Aggiornamento Educativo, Via Leone XIII 10, 20145, Milano (Tel: 39-2-481.83.31/Fax: 39-2-48.19.32.29).

The subnetwork's reflections have led to a comparative and descriptive study of the situation of handicapped children in the education systems of several member states, the development of a database to classify and list the most commonly used key-words related to aspects of special education, and to the preparation of a 'Guide to the education systems for handicapped children'.

Subnetwork 15: The European Dimension and Training the Trainers

France and Italy: Coordinated by the Institut européen pour le développement des potentialités des enfants (IEDPE), 12 rue Thouin, 75005 Paris (Tel: 33-1-46.33.38.56/Fax: 33-1-46.33.38. 56) and Dip. di Filosofia, Sez. di Psicologia e Pedagogia, Vico S. Antonio 5/7, 16100 Genova (Tel: 39-10-839.26.62).

Set up at the beginning of the academic year 1992–3 this subnetwork has as its objective the setting up of a European School for the training of teacher trainers. Such a school should not be seen as a building but as a network for European postgraduate training which can be delivered at different places and by different experts using the potential of teacher trainers available at European level, notably in the RIF.

Subnetwork 16: The European Dimension — Physical and Health Education

Germany: Coordinated by Universität Osnabrück, Fachbereich Erziehungs und kulturwissenschaften, Heger-Tar-Wall 9, 4500 Osnabrück (Tel: 49-541-969.42.51/Fax: 49-541-969.47.68).

This subnetwork was still in the process of formation at the time of the Leuven/Liège meeting though some preliminary cooperation between members has taken place through the bilateral exchanges carried out within the RIF.

European Questionnaire

This questionnaire was part of a research project carried out by Anne Convery, Michael Evans, Simon Green, Ernesto Macaro and Janet Mellow in 1993–4 involving 1200 teenagers aged 14–16 in England, France, Germany, the Netherlands and Spain.

It included a general knowledge quiz which covered areas of basic information about the European union, including geographical, financial and policy issues. Respondents were asked to indicate the truth or falsity of various statements such as:

- There are twelve member states of the European Community (EC).
- The ECU is worth less than 50p.
- The country with the largest population in the EC is Germany.
- The EC has the ultimate say in issues regarding road safety.
- The UK cannot send troops to fight in a war zone (e.g., Bosnia) without the consent of the European Parliament.
- The fall of the Berlin wall signified the end of World War II.

As these examples show, unlike similar European questionnaires, this model addressed the whole curriculum not just the subject of modern foreign languages.

European Organizations and Acronyms

EU Programmes

Comett
Rue Montoyer 14
1040 Bruxelles
(Tel: +32 2 513 89 59
 Fax: +32 2 513 9346)

Cooperation between universities and industry, including technology

Erasmus
Rue Montoyer 17
1040 Bruxelles
(Tel: +32 2 233 0111
Fax: +32 2 233 0150)

Mobility of university students including teachers in training

Eurotecnet
Rue des deux Eglises 38
1040 Bruxelles
(Tel: +32 2 209 1311)

Innovation in vocational training

Force
Rue du Nord 34
1000 Bruxelles
(Tel: +32 2 212 0411)

Promoting continuing vocational training

Helios Team
79 Avenue de Cortenberg
1040 Bruxelles
(Tel: +32 2 735 4105
Fax: +32 2 735 1671)

Integration of the disabled into the educational system

Iris
Rue de la Tourelle 21
1040 Bruxelles
(Tel: 32 2 230 5158)

Vocational training for women

Lingua
Rue du Commerce 10
1040 Bruxelles
(Tel: +32 2 511 4218)

Promoting language competence

Petra/Youth
Place du Luxembourg 2–3
1040 Bruxelles
(Tel: +32 2 511 1510
Fax: +32 2 511 1960)

Vocational training

Tempus
Avenue des Arts 19H
1040 Bruxelles
(Tel: +32 2 212 0411)

Programmes of assistance in the economic and social, including educational, restructuring of central and eastern European countries

Youth for Europe
Youth Exchange Centre
10 Spring Gardens
London SW1A 5BN
(Tel: 0171 389 4030
 Fax: 0171 389 4033)

Youth exchanges and out of school activities

Information Networks

Eurydice
Rue d'Arlon 15
1040 Bruxelles
(Tel: +32 2 238 3011)

Eurodesk
Central Bureau
Seymour Mews House
Seymour Mews
London WC1H 9PE
(Tel: 0171 725 5101)
Scottish Community Education Council
(Tel: 0131 313 2488)

European Education Research Trust
76 Alfriston Road
London SW11 6NW
(Tel: 0171 228 4157)

Epic (Europe Education Policy Information Centre)
NFER
The Mere
Upton Park
Slough
Berks., SL1 2DQ

Council for Cultural Cooperation
Directorate of Education Culture and Sport
Council of Europe
BP431 R6
67006
Strasbourg, CEDEX
(Tel: +33 88 41 2000
Fax: +33 88 41 2788)

Europe in the Round   Careers guidance for schools
Vocational Technologies Ltd
32 Castle Street
Guildford
GU1 3UW
(Tel: 01483 579454)

Careers Europe   Careers information in Europe
Ground Floor, Equity Chambers
40 Piccadilly
Bradford
BD1 3NN
(Tel: 01274 757521)

Central Bureau/United Kingdom Centre for European Education Publications

Edit
EuroedNews
European Awareness
The European Dimension in Education
Partner Schools Abroad
Schools Unit News

For Further information readers are referred to *Eurojargon*, a guide by Anne Ramsay to EU acronyms and abbreviations, Capital Planning Information. (Tel: 01789 57300; Fax: 01780 54333)

Bibliography

ADAMS, A. (1976) *The Humanities Jungle*, London, Ward Lock Educational.

ADAMS, A. (1991) 'Innovation in teacher education: The case of the PGCE', in PROTHEROUGH, R. and ATKINSON, J. *The Making of English Teachers*, Milton Keynes, Open University Press.

ADAMS, A. and HADLEY, E. (1982) 'A study in method — some aspects of the PGCE', in ADAMS, A. (Ed.) *New Directions in English Teaching*, Lewes, Falmer Press.

ADAMS, A. and TULASIEWICZ, W. (1992) 'A European dimension to intercultural education', in CONVEY, A. (Ed.) *Approaches to the European Dimension in Teacher Education*, London, Central Bureau for Educational Visits and Exchanges.

ADAMS, A., CONVEY, A., TAVERNER, D., TULASIEWICZ, W. and TURNER, K. (1992) *The Changing European Classroom: Multi-cultural Schooling and the New Europe*, Cambridge, University Department of Education.

ALEXANDER, R., ROSE, J. and WOODHEAD, C. (1992) 'Curriculum Organisation and Classroom Practice in primary schools' — a discussion paper, London, DES.

ALEXANDER, R. and WHITTAKER, J. (1980) *Developments in PGCE Courses*, Guildford, University of Surrey.

ALTRICHTER, H. and POSCH, P. (1989) 'Does the grounded theory approach offer a guiding paradigm for teacher researchers?', *Cambridge Journal of Education*, 19, 1, Cambridge, Institute of Education.

ASELMAIER, U., EIGENBRODT, K.-W., KRON, F.W. and VOGEL, G. (Eds) (1985) *Fachdidaktik am Scheideweg*, Munchen, E. Reinhardt.

ATL (1993) *The Education of a Profession*, London, Association of Teachers and Lecturers.

BARANGER, P. and BLAIS, M. (1993) 'La formation commune affiche son contenu', *Recherche et Formation*, 13, Paris, INRP.

BARNETT, C. (1986) *The Audit of War*, Macmillan, London.

BARRETT, E., BARTON, L., FURLONG, J., GALVIN, C., MILES, S. and WHITTY, G. (1992) *Initial Teacher Education in England and Wales: A Topography*, London, Goldsmiths' College/ESRC.

BARRETT, E. and GALVIN, C. (1993) *The Licensed Teacher Scheme*, London, Institute of Education.

BEARDON, T., BOOTH, M., HARGREAVES, D. and REISS, M. (1992) *School-Led Initial Teacher Training: The Way Forward*, Cambridge, University Department of Education.

BENNETT, N. and CARRÉ, C. (1993) *Learning to Teach*, London, Routledge.

BERIOT, A.-M. *et al.* (1992) 'La mise en place de IUFM-pilotes et le débat theorie-pratique', *Recherche et Formation*, 11, Paris, INRP.

BLACKLEDGE, R. (1982) 'Reflections and Observations on the CDCC Project', *Preparation for Life*, 1, Strasbourg, Council of Europe.

BOOTH, M., FURLONG, J. and WILKIN, M. (Eds) (1990) *Partnership in Initial Teacher Training*, London, Cassell.

BOURDONCLE, R. and CROS, F. (1989) 'Teacher preparation and the reform of collèges in France', in TULASIEWICZ, W. and ADAMS, A. (Eds) *Teachers' Expectations and Teaching Reality*, London, Routledge.

BOURDONCLE, R. and LOUVET, A. (Eds) (1991) 'Les Tendences Nouvelles dans la formation des enseignants: Strategies françaises et expériences étrangères', *Actes de colloque, Novembre, 1990*, Paris, INRP.

BROCKHAUS ENZYKLOPÄDIE (1990) Vol. 13, Mannheim, F A Brockhaus GmbH.

BROCK, C. and TULASIEWICZ, W. (Eds) (1994) *Education in a Single Europe*, London, Routledge.

BURGESS, T. (Ed.) (1971) *Dear Lord James: A Critique of Teacher Education*, Harmondsworth, Penguin Books.

CALDWELL, B. and CARTER, C. (1993) *The Return of the Mentor*, London, Falmer Press.

CHAIX, M.-L. (1992) 'Alternance et rapport theorie/pratique: un itineraire de réflexion', *Recherche et Formation*, 11, Paris, INRP.

CHILTON, P. and AUBREY, C. (Eds) (1983) *Nineteen Eighty-Four in 1984*, London, Comedia.

CHITTY, C. and SIMON, B. (1993) *Education Answers Back: Critical Responses to Government Policy*, London, Lawrence and Wishart.

CLANDININ, D. and CONNELLY, F. (1987) 'What is "Personal" in the studies of the personal?', *Journal of Curriculum Studies*, 19, 6.

COMMISSION OF THE EUROPEAN COMMUNITIES (1993), Green Paper [29 September 1993, COM(93) 457 final] on 'The European Dimension of Education', Brussels.

CONVEY, A. (Ed.) (1992) *Approaches to the European Dimension in Teacher Education*, London, Central Bureau for Educational Visits and Exchanges.

CONVEY, A. (1994) 'Teacher mobility and conditions of service in the European community', in TULASIEWICZ, W. and STROWBRIDGE, G. (Eds) *education and the Law*, London, Routledge.

CONVEY, F. (1992) 'The European dimension and the world of work', in CONVEY, A. (Ed.) *Approaches to the European Dimension in Teacher Education*, London, Central Bureau for Educational Visits and Exchanges.

CREMIN, L. (1988) *American Education: The Metropolitan Experience 1876–1980*, New York, Harper and Row.

DARLING-HAMMOND, L. (Ed.) (1994) *Developing Professional Development Schools: Schools for Developing a Profession*, New York, Teachers' College Press.

DEARING, R. (1993) *The National Curriculum and its Assessment — Final Report*, London, SCAA.

DEARING, R. (1994a) *Geography in the National Curriculum: Draft Proposals*, London, SCAA.

DEARING, R. (1994b) *History in the National Curriculum: Draft Proposals*, London, SCAA.

DES (1972) *Teacher Education and Training* (The James Report), London, HMSO.

DES (1982) *The New Teacher in School*, London, HMSO.

DES (1983) *White Paper: Teaching Quality*, Commd.8836, London, HMSO.

DES (1984) *Circular 3/84 — Initial Teacher Training: Approval of Courses*, London, DES.

DES (1988) *The New Teacher in School*, London, HMSO.

DES (1989a) *Perspectives on Teacher Education: Other Trainers' Views*, London, DES.

DES (1991a) *The European Dimension in Education: A Statement of the UK Government's Policy and Report of Activities*, London, HMSO.

DES (1991b) *Statistics of Education: Teachers in Service in England and Wales 1989 and 1990*, London, HMSO.

DES (1991c) *School-based Initial Teacher Training in England and Wales*. A report by HM Inspectorate, London, HMSO.

DFE (1992) *Circular 9/92: Initial Teacher Training* (Secondary Phase), London, DFE.

DFE (1993) *The Administration and Funding of Initial Teacher Training: The Government's Proposals for the Reform of Initial Teacher Training*, London, DFE.

DEPARTMENT OF EDUCATION NORTHERN IRELAND (1992) *Educational Themes*, Belfast, HMSO.

EAT (European Association for Teachers) and ERGTSE (European Group on Training for Teacher Exchanges) (1993) *Teaching for Exchanges — Aims and Ways of Teacher Training*, Strasbourg, Council of Europe Press.

ELLIOTT, J. (Ed.) (1993) *Restructuring Teacher Education*, London, Falmer Press.

FARREN, S. (1994) 'Language, Education and Society in a Changing World', unpublished paper presented at the IRAAL Conference, Dublin.

FURLONG, V.J., HIRST, P.H., POCKLINGTON, K. and MILES, S. (1988) *Initial Teacher Training and the Role of the School*, Milton Keynes, Open University Press.

GALVIN, C. (1994) 'Lessons unlearnt? Aspects of training licensed teachers', in REID, I., GRIFFITHS, R. and CONSTABLE, H. (Eds) *Teacher Education Reform: Current Research*, London, Paul Chapman.

GILMOUR, I. (1992) *Dancing with Dogma*, London, Simon and Schuster.

GOODLAD, J. (1991) 'Why we need a complete redesign of teacher education', in BRANDT, R. *On Teacher Education: A Conversation With John Goodlad, Educational Leadership*, 49, New York.

GUMBERT, E. (1990) *Fit to Teach: Teacher Education in International Perspective*, Atlanta, Georgia State University.

HAKE, C. (1993) *Partnership in Initial Teacher Training: Talk and Chalk*, London, Tufnell Press.

HALSTEAD, M. (1988) *Education, Justice and Cultural Diversity: An Examination of the Honeyford Affair, 1984–85*, London, Falmer Press.

HAMBURGER, F. (1991) 'Einwanderung in die Bundesrepublik Deutschland Anforderungen der multikulturellen Gesellschaft', in KIND-JUGEND-GESELLSCHAFT, *Zeitschrift für Jugendschutz*, 36, No. 2.

HAMBURGER, F. (1994) *Pädagogik der Einwanderungsgesellschaft*, Frankfurt am Main, Cooperative-Verlag.

HARGREAVES, D. (1990) *The Future of Teacher Education*, Hockerill, Hockerill Educational Foundation.

HARGREAVES, D. (1994) *The Mosaic of Learning*, London, DEMOS.

HENRY, N. (Ed.) (1993) *Education for the Professions*, Chicago, University of Chicago Press.

HILLCOLE GROUP (1993) *Whose Teachers? A Radical Manifesto*, London, Tufnell Press, paper 9.

HIRST, P. (1976) 'The PGCE course: Its objectives and their nature', *British Journal of Teacher Education*, 2, 1, London, Methuen.

HIRST, P. (1990) 'The theory-practice relationship in teacher training', in BOOTH, M., FURLONG, J. and WILKIN, M. (Eds) *Partnership in Initial Teacher Training*, London, Cassell.

HIRST, P. (1993) 'Education, knowledge and practices', in BARROW, R. and WHITE, P. (Eds) *Beyond Liberal Education*, London, Routledge.

HMI (1988) *Education Observed No. 7. Initial Teacher Training*, London, DES.

HMI (1989a) *The Provisional Teacher Programme in New Jersey*, London, HMSO.

HMI (1989b) *Initial Teacher Training in France*, London, HMSO.

HMI (1991a) *School based Initial Teacher Training in England and Wales*, London, HMSO.

HMI (1991b) *A Survey of the International Baccalaureate: Autumn 1989 and Spring 1990*, London, DES.

HMI (1992) *The Annual Report of HM Senior Chief Inspector of Schools: Education in England 1990–1991*, London, DES.

HOLMES GROUP INC. (1986) *Tomorrow's Teachers: A Report of the Holmes Group*, East Lansing, College of Education Michigan State University.

HOLMES GROUP INC. (1990) *Tomorrow's Schools: Principles for the Design of Professional Development Schools*, East Lansing, Michigan.

HOUSE OF COMMONS (1990) *Report of the Commission on Citizenship: Encouraging Citizenship*, London, HMSO.

JANSSENS, S. and LOLY-SMETS, R. (Eds) (1994) *Report of the RIF European Symposium '93 of the Network of Teacher Training Institutions*, Leuven.

JUDGE, H. (1982) *American Graduate Schools of Education: A View from Abroad*, New York, Ford Foundation.

JUDGE, H. (1992) *American Graduate Schools of Education: A View from Abroad*, New York, Ford Foundation.

KELCHTERMANS, G. (1994) 'Recent European Research on Teacher Training and Professional Development', in JANSSENS, S. and LOLY-SMETS, R. (Eds) *Report of the RIF European Symposium '93 of the Network of Teacher Training Institutions*, Leuven.

KING, A. and REISS, M. (Eds) (1993) *The Multicultural Dimension of the National Curriculum*, London, Falmer Press.

KODRON, C. (1993) 'European dimension, multiculturalism and teacher training: An experience in a network of training institutions', *European Journal of Teacher Education*, 16, 1, Abingdon, Carfax.

KROATH, F. (1989) 'How do Teachers change their practical theories?', *Cambridge Journal of Education*, 19, 1, Cambridge, Institute of Education.

KRON, F.W. (1988) *Grundwissen Pädagogik*, Munich and Basle, Ernst Reinhardt.

KRON, F.W. (1989) 'The nature and limitations of teachers' professional autonomy', in TULASIEWICZ, W. and ADAMS, A. (1989) *Teachers' Expectations and Teaching Reality*, London, Routledge.

KRON, F.W. (1993) *Grundwissen Didaktik*, Munich and Basle, Ernst Reinhardt.

KRON, F.W. (1994) 'Germany', in BROCK, C. and TULASIEWICZ, W. *Education in a Single Europe*, London, Routledge.

LACY, C. and LAMONT, W. (1976) 'Partnership with schools', *British Journal of Teacher Education*, 2, 1, London, Methuen.

LAWLOR, S. (1990) *Teachers Mistaught: Training in Theories or Education in Subjects?*, London, Centre for Policy Studies.

LAWTON, D. (1984) *The Tightening Grip: Growth of Central Control of the School Curriculum*, London, University of London Institute of Education [Bedford Way Paper No. 21].

LAWTON, D. (1992) *Education and Politics in the 1990s: Conflict or Consensus?*, London, Falmer Press.

LAWTON, D. and GORDON, P. (1987) London, Routledge and Kegan Paul.

MACDONALD, B. (1984) *Teacher Education and Curriculum Reform: Some English Errors*, Valencia, address to Spanish teacher trainers.

MCINTYRE, D., HAGGER, H. and WILKIN, M. (1993) *Mentoring: Perspectives on School-Based Education*, London, Kogan Page.

McLaughlin, G. (1994) *'All Day Game' and 'Business Game'*, London, The Federal Trust.

McLean, M. (1990) *Britain and a Single Market Europe: Prospects for a Common School Curriculum*, London, Kogan Page.

McLean, M. (1992) *The Promise and Perils of Educational Comparison*, London, Tufnell Press.

McNair Report (1944) *The Training of Teachers and Youth Leaders*, London, HMSO.

Mead, M. (1970) *Culture and Commitment*, New York and London, Doubleday.

Ministere de l'education (1993) *Documentation française 1992 and 1993: Rapport de l'inspection générale de l'éducation nationale*, Paris, Ministère de l'éducation nationale.

Mitter, W. (1989) 'Recent trends in educational policies in the Federal Republic of Germany', in Tulasiewicz, W. and Adams, A. (Eds) *Teachers' Expectations and Teaching Reality*, London, Routledge.

Munro, R.G. (1993) 'A case study of school-based training systems in New Zealand secondary schools', in Elliott, J. *Restructuring Teacher Education*, London, Falmer Press.

NCC (1991) *The National Curriculum and Student, Articled and Licensed Teachers*, York, NCC.

NUT (1992) *A Statement of the National Union of Teachers in Response to the Government's Proposal for the Reform of Initial Teacher Training*, London, Hamilton House.

O'Hear, A. (1988) *Who Teaches the Teachers? A contribution to Public Debate of the DES Green Paper*, London, Social Affairs Unit.

OFSTED (1993) The Secondary PGCE in Universities, London: HMSO.

Orwell, G. (1946), 'Politics and the English language' in Horizon, April 1946; reprinted in (1968) *The Collected Essays, Journalism and Letters of George Orwell*, 4, London, Secker and Warburg.

Peck, B. and Sutherland, I. (1991) *Working as a Teacher in Scotland*, Glasgow, Jordanhill College of Education.

PETRA (1993) *Vademecum, 1994* Luxembourg, Commission of the European Communities.

Plowden Lady (1967) *Children and their Primary Schools* (The Plowden Report), London, HMSO.

Roche, M. (1993) *Rethinking Citizenship*, Cambridge, Polity Press.

Ross, A.M. and Tomlinson, S. (1991) *Teachers for Tomorrow, Education and Training, Paper No. 7*, London, Institute for Public Policy Research.

Schmidt-Bleibtreu, B. and Klein, F. (1973) *Kommentar zum Grundgesetz für die Bundesrepublik Deutschland*, 3rd Edition, Neuwied and Berlin, Luchterhand Verlag.

Schön, D. (1983) *The Reflective Practitioner*, London, Temple Smith.

Schryver, R. De (1994) 'The historical perspective of the work of the RIF sub-network', in JANSSENES, S. and LOLY-SMETS, R. (Eds) *Report of the RIF European Symposium '93 of the Network of Teacher Training Institutions*, Leuven.

SCOTTISH CONSULTATIVE COUNCIL ON THE CURRICULUM (1993) *Thinking European: Ideas for Integrating a European Dimension into the Curriculum*, Dundee, Scottish CCC.

SHAW, R. (1992) *Teacher Training in Secondary Schools*, London, Kogan Page.

SHENNAN, M. (1991) *Teaching about Europe*, London, Council of Europe and Cassell.

SIMON, B. (1976) 'Theoretical aspects of the PGCE course', *British Journal of Teacher Education*, 2, 1, London, Methuen.

SIMON, B. (1994) *What Future for Education?*, London, Lawrence and Wishart.

SLEE, B. (1991) 'L'Education civique en Grande Bretagne. Citoyenneté et éducation', *La Formation du futur citoyen par le droit dans les collèges*, Paris, Laboratoire de Sociologie Juridique, Université Panthéon-Assas-CRNS.

SOLTIS, J. (1987) *Reforming Teacher Education: The Impact of the Holmes Group*, New York, Teachers' College Press.

SPEAKER'S COMMISSION (1990) *Report of the Commission on Citizenship: 'Encouraging Citizenship'*, London, HMSO.

STANLEY, W.B. (1992) *Curriculum for Utopia*, New York, State University of New York Press.

STROWBRIDGE, G. (1994) 'Law and vocational education, and training of 16 to 19 year olds: The English experience since 1979', in TULASIEWICZ, W. and STROWBRIDGE, G. (1994) *Education and the Law*, London, Routledge.

TOMLINSON, J. (1993) *The Control of Education*, London, Cassell.

TOURNIER, M. (1993) *La formation des instituteurs a l'université et ses conséquences: le cas dea République fédérale d'Allemagne*, Paris, INRP.

TULASIEWICZ, W. (1986) 'Interdisciplinary tutor-led discussion groups in the new pattern of teacher education in England', *European Journal of Teacher Education*, 9, 2, Abingdon, Carfax.

TULASIEWICZ, W. (1993a) 'The European dimension and the National Curriculum', in KING, A. and REISS, M. (Eds) *The Multicultural Dimension of the National Curriculum*, London, Falmer Press.

TULASIEWICZ, W. (1993b) 'Knowledge about Language/Language Awareness: A new dimension in school languages curriculum', *Curriculum and Teaching*, 8, 1, Melbourne, James Nicholson.

TULASIEWICZ, W. (1994) 'Education for citizenship: School life and society: British-European Comparisons', in TULASIEWICZ, W. and STROWBRIDGE, G. (Eds) *Education and the Law*, London, Routledge.

TULASIEWICZ, W. and ADAMS, A. (Eds) (1989) *Teachers' Expectations and Teaching Reality*, London, Routledge.

TULASIEWICZ, W., ADAMS, A. and HARGREAVES, D. (1992) 'Un débat anglais prémonitoire: l'établissement scolaire et la formation', *Recherche et Formation*, 12, Paris, INRP.

TULASIEWICZ, W. and STROWBRIDGE, G. (1994) *Education and the Law*, London, Routledge.

TULASIEWICZ, W. and TAVERNER, D. (1989) 'Entstehung und Ende des Schools Council for Curriculum and Examinations', *Bildung und Erziehung*, 42, 2, Köln, Böhlau.

TULASIEWICZ, W. and TO, CH. Y. (1993) *World Religions and Educational Practice*, London, Cassell.

TURNEY, C., CAIRNS, L., ELTIS, K., HATTON, N., THEW, D., TOWLER, J. and WRIGHT, R. (1982) *Supervisor Development Programmes — Role Handbook*, Sydney, Sydney University Press.

TURNEY, C., ELTIS, K., TOWLER, J. and WRIGHT, R. (1985) *The Practicum Curriculum: A New Basis for Teacher Education*, Sydney, Sydney Academic Press.

UNESCO AND THE INTERNATIONAL BUREAU OF EDUCATION (1975) *Working Documents at the 35th session of the International Conference on Education: — The Changing Role of the Teacher*, Geneva, UNESCO.

WALTON, J. (1993) *Learning to Succeed: Report of the National Commission on Education*, London, Heinemann.

WELBERS, G. (1993) 'PETRA's Added Value', *PETRA Yearbook 1992–93*, Brussels, Commission for the European Communities.

WHITTY, G. *et al.* (1992) 'Initial teacher education in England and Wales: A survey of current practices and concerns', *Cambridge Journal of Education*, 22, 3, Cambridge, Institute of Education.

WILKIN, M. (Ed.) (1992) *Mentoring in Schools*, London, Kogan Page.

WILKIN, M. and SANKEY, D. (Eds) (1994) *Collaboration and Transition in Initial Teacher Training*, London, Kogan Page.

Williams, D. (1994) 'Preface', in TULASIEWICZ, W. and STROWBRIDGE, G. (Eds) *Education and the Law*, London, Routledge.

WRIGHT, P., McGIBBON, M. and WALTON, P. (1989) *The Effectiveness of the Teacher Training Programme*, Sacramento, California: Commission on Teacher Credentialing.

Index

Adams, A., 42, 47, 66–7, 70, 107, 123
Alexander and Whittaker, 23
ARION, 91
Aselmaier *et al.*, 7
Assessment, 36, 142–3
Australia, 43

Barrett *et al.*, 34
Batchelor of Education (BEd), 17, 33
Belgium, 110, 148, 149
Bolton, E., 32
British Association of Teachers and Researchers in Overseas Education (BATROE), 83
Burgess, T., 22

Caldwell and Carter, 30–1
Cambridge, University of, 23, 26, 33, 45, 49, 106, 146
Careers, 9, 156
CEDEFOP, see European entries
Centre for Policy Studies, 11, 23, 32
Chitty and Simon, 21, 32
City Technology Colleges, 30
Civil Servant, 61–9, 71, 84
Committee of Vice-Chancellors and Principals (CVPC), ix, 29, 63
COMETT, 92, 154
competences, 28, 140, 141, 145
comprehensive schools, 8, 58
Confederation of British Industry (CBI), ix
Conservative Party, 11, 14, 20, 25
Convey, F., 125–6, 128
Council for the accreditation of Teacher Education (CATE), 17, 28, 29, 47, 65, 72, 87, 106, 146
Council for Cultural Co-operation, 156
Crowther Report (1959), 120
Curriculum, xi, 23, 27, 37, 41, 63, 69, 70, 72, 99, 116, 117, 122, 124, 125, 128, 134, 140, 145

Darling-Hammond, L., 79, 80
Dearing Report, 8, 21, 111, 113, 115–7
Denmark, 150
Department of Education and Science (DES), 4, 5, 6, 7, 27, 28, 47, 64, 68, 106, 114
Department for Education (DFE), 15, 17, 18, 35, 38, 40, 47, 57, 139

Education Acts
    1870, 19
    1944, ix, 17, 27
    Reform 1988, 5, 10, 65
    1993, 25
educational reform, 70–2, 73, 133
educational theory, xi, 11, 24, 74–9
Eggleston, J., 11
Elementary-school teaching, 6, 7
Elliott, J., 50–1
England and Wales, ix, 13, 16, 23, 31, 33, 36–8, 43, 48, 57, 58, 62–8, 70–2, 75–8, 80–7, 100, 103, 105, 106, 107–17, 129, 131, 133–5, 139, 146, 150, 153
ERASMUS programme, 91–8, 103, 147, 149, 150, 151, 154
Ethnic-minority groups, 107–9
Eurodesk, 155
European Centre for the Development of Vocational Training (CEDEFOP), 91
Europe Education Policy Information Centre (EPIC), 156
Europe, 9, 13, 37, 46, 51, 56, 58, 59, 63, 64, 66, 69, 70, 72, 73–4, 75, 80–6, 91, 92, 107–17, 118–32, 133–5, 139, 146, 153
European Credit Transfer System (ECTS), 95, 104

Index

Europe in the Round, 156
European Union (Community,
    Treaty of), 4, 36, 38, 68, 91, 92,
    94, 95–106, 107–17, 137–8,
    147–52, 153, 154–6
Eurotecnet, 154
EURYDICE, 91, 97, 155

Federal Trust, 107, 110
Force, 154
France, viii, ix, 13, 39, 56, 57, 60–7,
    71–6, 82, 85, 86, 103, 107, 109,
    114, 116, 117, 147, 151, 153
Furlong, V.J., 40, 83

Galvin, C., 34
General Teaching Council (GTC,
    Scotland), 38, 58, 78, 86, 102,
    103, 139
Germany, viii, ix, 4–6, 12, 30, 31,
    57, 61–7, 73–9, 81–7, 107–10,
    112, 116–7, 128, 133, 134, 151–3
Grant maintained schools (GM), 10, 30
Greece, 8, 150

Hargreaves, D., x, 50–1, 66, 82
Helios team, 154
Higher Education Institutions (HEI),
    16, 18–20, 22, 23, 28–30, 35–40,
    42–8, 50, 57, 66, 67, 72–88, 98,
    112, 127, 131, 140
Hillcole Group, 19
Hirst, P., 23–4, 51, 77
Holmes proposals, x, 79

Independent schools, 8, 30, 32
Initial teacher education (ITT), 22, 27,
    28, 30, 32–5, 37, 40, 41, 43, 47,
    48, 63–4, 83, 92
In-service education for teaching
    (INSET), 22, 23, 34, 48, 71, 76,
    83, 101, 126, 128, 131
Inspectorate, Her Majesty's (HMI),
    viii, 10, 17, 18, 27, 32, 34, 47,
    58, 66
International Baccalaureate (IB)
    Ireland, 148
    IRIS, 154
    Italy, 151
Institut Universitaire de formation des
    Maitres (IUFM), 56, 60, 63, 71,
    73, 75, 78, 80, 85, 147

James report, 22–4, 48

Kron, F.W., 76, 77, 116

Labour Party, 16
Lawlor, S., 20, 32, 58
Lawton, D., 62, 66, 87
LEONARDO DA VINCI
    (LEONARDO), 94, 99, 111,
    123, 124, 128
Lerman, C., 26
Licensed teachers' scheme, 34–5, 58
LINGUA, 92, 94–5, 155
Local Education Authorities (LEAs),
    37, 38, 51, 66, 86, 98, 115
Local Management of Schools (LMS),
    10, 23, 37, 48, 51, 72

Maastricht Treaty, viii, 83, 91, 104,
    129, 137
Macdonald, B., 41–2, 49, 51
McLean, M., viii, 112–3
Mead, M., 42
Mentoring, 30–1, 35, 38, 39, 42–3,
    49, 81–2
Methods, xi, 3, 6, 15, 45–6, 48, 49,
    122
Modes of Teacher Education Project
    (MOTE), 34–7
Moon, Bob, 39–40

National Commission on Education,
    18
National Curriculum, 20–1, 35–7, 51,
    63, 84, 103, 113–4, 116, 129,
    140, 142
National Curriculum Council, 63,
    105, 109, 114
Nation state, 4, 12, 65, 69
Netherlands, 59, 149, 153

Office for Standards of Education
    (OFSTED), viii, 17, 27, 66, 76,
    86, 87, 146
Open University, 38–40

Partnership, 24, 29, 30, 43–4, 46,
    78–80
PETRA, 92, 98, 104, 129, 155
Poland, ix, 4, 8, 40, 61, 64, 67, 71–3,
    75–6, 82, 85, 86, 134
Portugal, 9, 127, 147, 149
Postgraduate Certificate of Education,
    72, 86–7, 120
Practical preparation, *see* Teaching
    practice

166

Primary education, 28, 35
Professional Development School (PDS), x, 75, 79–81, 88
Professional Tutors, 76, 81–3
Programmes, European, 91–8, 102–6
Prussia, 7, 8

Qualified Teacher Status (QTS), 47, 86
quality, 26, 27, 31, 70, 72, 97, 104, 134

Religious education, 8, 10, 64, 69, 86
RIF (Network of Training Institutions), 92–3, 98, 100, 106, 129, 130, 147–52

Schön, D., 24, 28, 67, 82
School-based training, x, 15, 17, 37, 48, 50
School Centred Initial Teacher Training Schemes (SCITT), 44–5
School curriculum, 7–8, 9–10, 61, 62, 66, 105, 111, 113, 116
Schools Council for Curriculum and Examinations (SCCE), 87, 121
School Curriculum and Assessment Authority (SCAA), 63, 109
School Examinations and Assessment Council (SEAC), 63
Scotland, ix, 8, 9, 13n., 16, 22, 34, 37, 38, 58, 67, 68, 75–6, 78, 86, 102–3, 112, 115, 128, 139, 141–2, 148
secondary schooling, 6, 55, 133
Simon, B., viii, 24, 51, 77
SOCRATES programme, 92–3, 94–101, 103, 106, 114, 123, 124, 128, 147

Spain, 148, 153
State-maintained schools, 7
Status of teachers, 7, 67–9

Teacher education, 3–4, 6, 7, 9–11, 12, 14, 17–9, 22, 24–8, 31, 33, 35–40, 43–6, 48, 55, 59, 63–4, 66, 71, 80, 93, 98, 103–6, 118–32, 133–4
Teacher preparation, x, xi, 8–9, 11–13, 55–6, 59–60, 62, 64–5, 67, esp. 71–88, 98–101, 118–32, 133–4
concurrent model, 56–7, 69
consecutive model, 56–7, 69
Teacher-training, 7, 10, 19, 24, 32, 36, 69, 140–4
Teacher Training Agency (TTA), ix, 14–16, 27–8, 31, 37, 44, 60, 72, 75, 81, 87, 146
Teacher Unions, 13, 16, 40–1, 43–4, 60, 67, 86, 131
Teaching practice, 33, 47, 48, 74–7
Tempus, 155
Testing, 11, 65
Tomlinson, J., 62, 87
Tulasiewicz, W., 9, 21, 23, 50, 64, 66, 70, 71, 87, 105, 110, 122, 127
Turner, K., 126–7

University Council for Education in Teaching (UCET), 23, 63
United States of America, 31, 64, 67, 69, 78, 82, 86, 88, 112

Youth for Europe, 155

R